Sales: The Mind's Side

What They Never Taught You In Sales Training

James E. Robertson

Metamorphous Press
Portland, Oregon

Published by

Metamorphous Press
P.O. Box 10616
Portland, OR 97210-0616

Copyright © 1990 by James E. Robertson
Cover Art, Book Design & Editing by Lori Stephens
Printed in the United States

Robertson, James E., 1945-
Sales: the mind's side /
by James E. Robertson
p. cm.
Includes bibliographical references.
ISBN 1-55552-006-5 : $12.95
1. Selling. I. Title
HF5438.25.R59   1989
658.8—dc20   89-12922

This book is set in 11 pt. ITC New Baskerville,
formatted with Xerox Ventura Publisher® and Aldus
PageMaker®, and output on a Linotronic L-300 imagesetter.

Contents

iv

Publisher's Preface

You are holding a very special book for the sales professional. James Robertson has tied together the "grass roots" aspects of selling and identifies sales more as a whole body process, rather than a set of closing techniques.

In the area of human performance, Robertson's working knowledge has been enhanced by the work he and his firms have done with professional athletes and coaches. Through personal experience, he has found that the world of sports has a lot to teach the business community about leadership, motivation, and even salesmanship.

NeuroLinguistic Programming is a practical and powerful model of human patterns of behavior and communication. It is a systematic study of observable patterns of behavior and communication and the processes that underlie them. This book includes some of the basic principles of NLP and demonstrates how this technology can improve any business person's success.

This blend of visualization, understanding the customer, NeuroLinguistic Programming, and whole body involvement from sports training truly makes this one of the most unique books on sales you are likely to ever read. Enjoy your journey.

Foreword

There Is No Need For Just "Another" Sales Book

We were all prepared to deliver a two-day sales training program for a major insurance company in southwest Florida. The date had been booked for months, the director of marketing and sales had set the agenda very precisely, and forty-six salespeople were scheduled to arrive in one week's time. A week before the training began, we got an excited call from the director of marketing about a new sales book the company had introduced at a corporate meeting in Chicago. "Can you change what we had planned to cover in the sales training program and teach this NEW SALES BOOK?" requested the excited sales director. With all of the confidence of someone who did not know any better, we told him certainly, if he could get a copy of the book up to us overnight. We silently said to ourselves, "No way! We will look through the book and teach what we had planned to cover in the first place."

After reading through this NEW SALES BOOK, a nagging thought hit us. The book really was not any different than what we were going to present in the first place. The cover was different, the author's method and style of writing were different, and the situations were specific for the insurance business. But this was NOT a new sales book. And if the book was not new, then there was certainly nothing new or unique about our own sales training program.

Even this revelation was not a sufficient wake-up call for us, and few major changes were made in either the content or the psychology of our existing sales training program. It was not until my firm began working with professional athletes that I realized what was wrong with our sales training program.

In going back through all of the sales books on my shelf, it became frightfully evident that there was not much new being written on the topic of selling since Willie Gayle's book, *Power Selling,* in 1959. His is a classic sales book for the 1950's.

We in the sales training community were not taking advantage of the work being done in areas of consumer buying habits by individuals including Dr. Roger Blackwell at Ohio State University, or of work being accomplished in the area of changing human behavior by people such as Ken Blanchard of the Blanchard Management Company in California. Why weren't people taking books like Dr. James Loehr's *Mental Toughness Training For Sports* and making the transition from sports to the profession of sales? In answering that question, *Sales: The Mind's Side* has three primary objectives:

1. To help you begin to view, understand, and work at selling from more of a buyer's perspective.

2. To help you apply the technological breakthroughs made in the areas of sports, psychology, and management to your own career in sales.

3. To support you in your own efforts to be a more effective learner, self-coach, and professional salesperson.

This is not JUST ANOTHER SALES BOOK.

Introduction

To Your Success
In The Balanced Approach
To Sales Success

Traditionally, the process of training, developing, and managing salespeople has focused almost entirely on sales techniques. Techniques have been treated separately from, and as superior to, the other mental and physical aspects of both the sales process and of the salesperson as an individual, and from the process of buying.

My own experience in sales developed through the stages of being an Assistant Professor of Business, an international sales and buying representative in Asia, a sales representative and manager for Burroughs Computers, a sales representative and training manager for AT&T-Southwestern Bell Telephone, and finally as the head of marketing for my own firms.

No place is the separation of mental from physical techniques more evident than in the world of amateur and professional sports. I mention this only because if it had not been for the chapter in my career that was written while I was president of the sports training firms of Sports Enhancement Associates and then Performance Enhancement Inc., the experience base for this book would never have evolved.

In our role as sports trainers, we surveyed over a

hundred top amateur and professional athletes as to how important the mental aspects of their performance were to their total performance. A majority of those surveyed responded in the 70% to 90% range for the importance of the mental aspects. When these same athletes were asked to describe their practice routines, close to 100% of their routines were based on physical technique improvement, not mental processing skills. When they were questioned as to how, and with what frequency, they practiced skills for the mental side of their success, no significant response was obtained, only wondering generalities.

With this information from amateur and professional athletes in hand, we began asking the same questions of the participants in our sales and sales management training programs. The results were virtually the same. Both salespeople and athletes alike realized that to a large extent their individual success was based on mental skills and capacities. But exactly what are these "mental" skills? How are they obtained and refined? How are they practiced and improved upon? Can "mental" skills be learned or are salespeople simply born with them?

These are the types of questions this book has been designed to help you develop answers to. All of the answers are available. It comes as no surprise to you that there are dimensions to sales other than sales techniques. As important as your sales techniques are, you have always known that they are but one element in your total formula for success. When you have experienced peak levels of performance in sales, or in other areas of your life such as athletics, you knew that special feeling. If you have not experienced that level of performance in your sales career, then you have missed the experience of a lifetime and it is truly an experience to be worked toward.

Science now tells us how closely related the areas of "mental" and "physical" performance are to each other, much like your own heart and brain. Your heart and brain are equally important in their total contribution to your health and life, yet each has separate and distinct functions. This being the case, which of the two organs is the more important in its role? The answer: take either organ out and see just how long you survive! Each is equally important and must work with the other.

Extensive research has revealed that all areas of your being—mental, physical, technical, and spiritual—must be attended to if you are to achieve the highest possible level of sales performance. Sales techniques and mental skills go together; they are one; they are a "goes with."

Another objective of this book is to help you recognize that a new dimension to sales exists and to help you cross traditional lines of performance and graduate to peak levels. If you have already experienced peak levels of performance in sales, the techniques in this book will support your performing in that mode more often and for prolonged periods of time. If you have not performed at that level, this book can be your guide to initial peak level performance.

Athletes the world over step back onto the field for their sport just to return to this higher level of performance, if only for a moment. Athletes are not alone in their desire to repeat the experience of success with mental training techniques. Their counterparts in business recount every rare moment when they have performed their respective tasks at peak levels.

Experiences at the higher level of performance may have been rare and brief for you in the past because, as a society, we have generally bought into a belief system that all to often denies that such an advanced level of performance even exists, and our belief systems are the essence of how we define "reality." In our current environment and support systems, there is all to often more support for failure than for success. Our language does not even support our living, working, selling, and playing in this higher dimension of performance. Therefore, one of the things we work toward accomplishing throughout this book is to help you develop a new vocabulary to better support your experiences with mental skills development.

There is little need to magnify the problems associated with under performance and negative life styles. The problem magnifies itself in the reflections of our daily lives. Not only does our performance in sales suffer, but our performance in life falters as well. Our increasing stress levels show up in every aspect of our lives, business, and personal wellness and happiness. Heart problems remain on the increase, divorce rates continue to climb, employment turnover rates within the sales industry remain high, and we have become more spectators of fun and enjoyment than participants.

There is another side to peak levels of performance and a balanced life, and this book is dedicated to your journey back to that dimension.

You may have bought some of the great lies that keep you from selling effectively and at peak levels. We will help you identify and correct those misconceptions. You have also been presented with misinformation and been allowed to fail and fall short of performing at peak levels. That is why this is not a book for you to read, but rather a book for you to do. There is an answer out there and you are it.

Beyond physical, beyond mental, YOU ARE STILL THE ANSWER.

1

Getting Back To The Experience

Sales Performance and Peak Performance

Bill Russell stepped back onto the basketball court in Boston Garden for one reason that night. Many years later he was to recall that it was not to win, lose, or even to play the basketball game that was scheduled. It was to get back into the "magic." He called it magic because he knew of no other words to describe it. He came to think of that special playing condition not as physical, not as mental, but magic.

What was so special about that magical state that Bill could not talk about it with his coach or teammates? What was there to talk about when there were no words for him to describe it? And what significance does the event have for your sales career? To Bill Russell, the basketball star, the state existed, he had been there, and it was real. When he was playing at this peak level of performance, there was no other game or feeling like it in the world. Sometimes other teammates would move into this mental state with him, and on very rare nights even players on the opposing team would move into the magic. But the moments were rare and much too far apart to please Bill Russell.

Is Bill Russell the only athlete to ever experience the magic? Far from it. In May, 1984, professional golfer Peter Jacobsen walked into a dimly lit room, put on a set of headphones, then laid down on a couch while two men flipped dials on a machine that played electronic tones. Peter had been winless on the very competitive professional golf tour for almost four years. The very week after training and working with electronic tones and advanced imagery training, Peter traveled to Texas, experienced a peak level of performance, and won the Colonial National Golf Tournament.

Salespeople And The Peak Level of Performance

Salespeople around the world have selectively experienced the same magic as basketball player Bill Russell, PGA golf professional Peter Jacobsen, and hundreds of other top athletes. In the world of athletics it may be called "shooting the lights out." In the world of sales it may be called "having one of those great days." Both groups are experiencing their own peak levels of performance.

What the trainers in the dimly lit room had been able to do was teach pro golfer Peter Jacobsen how to perform at peak levels, and more importantly, how to sustain that level of performance over time. The experiences of these athletes, and of business professionals just like them, were a driving force behind the writing of this book. Professionals around the world, in both sales and athletics, are being trained more and more at a conscious level to reach and sustain peak levels of performance.

This book can guide you, the salesperson, through the same journey. Professional athletes may say they were "playing out of their minds," and salespeople might have their best day and comment that they were "on a roll you would not believe," but they are all attempting to express the same EXPERIENCE. What they experienced was a superior level of performance, and it was an actual experience, not Bill Russell's magic.

Ask yourself a question. When salespeople say something like, "Man, was I selling out of my mind today," just whose mind do they think they were selling out of? What do they do, just climb into the mind of the greatest salesperson they know and sell out of their mind for a few minutes a day?

Part of the difficulty in talking and writing about this "other side" of performance, and there is another side to performance, is the lack of words to describe it. One of the most famous golfers of our time expressed her experience on the "other side" this way . . .

> "When I play my best golf, I feel as if I'm in a fog . . . standing back watching the earth in orbit with a golf club in my hand."
> — Mickey Wright, *Golf Digest*, 1981

What To Expect From This Book

One of my sales managers used to also accuse me of "selling in a fog," but this is not what we are talking about. If you have been in sales for very long, you have more than likely experienced the rare feeling of exhilaration described above.

Selling on the "other side" includes a sense that you can do no wrong, that all of the elements in the sales process are working together, that you are in total control, and that you can enjoy watching the sales process unfold successfully and completely. With that type of experience in mind here is what you can expect to gain from DOING this book:

- 1. An implementation map for your journey into the "other side" of peak performance in sales;
- 2. Mental and physical techniques (you will soon learn that these two words hold much the same meaning) to support your selling at those peak levels;
- 3. Sales techniques that support your mental processes and that more accurately identify the way your customers process information and make purchase decisions;
- 4. A process for making your existing sales techniques more consistent and productive because yes, sales techniques are important;
- 5. Techniques for changing your own behavior and for becoming your own best sales coach.

There is no magic, no short cut, no easy road to success. What exists is a structure for a plan, your plan, and a guide along your journey to the "other side" of sales performance.

Learning From Experience

Learning a new approach to sales is similar to the way you eat. You take a bite, chew on it for awhile, determine if you like it, and then make a choice. If you do not like it, you may choose to spit it out, or just not take another bite. When you like the taste, the process does not end with the chewing because food does not do your body any good until it is swallowed and ingested into your system.

To be of value to your personal success in sales, the material in this book is much the same as food. You have to take the information, chew on it for awhile, determine how it tastes to you, swallow if you like it, and then allow it to be ingested into the rest of your sales experience base. In sales performance, your EXPERIENCE BASE OF SUCCESS is key to future success.

Take A Drive In Your Dream Car

We have already stated that peak performance in selling is not made up of words alone, it is carved out of effective and appropriate experiences. So let's experience what you have just been reading about and let's ensure that we both know what we are talking about when we use the term "experience."

Mentally you are about to begin driving down the road in your new dream car. And this is not your father's Oldsmobile! What a great car. Take a minute right now and notice the color and style of the dream car you will be driving.

PLEASE DO NOW . . .

Close your eyes and notice the color of your car. Notice the kind or brand of car it is. Now, mentally sit inside your car and notice the texture of its seats. Start your car and begin driving down the road slowly.

Experience the feel of the road as you ride quietly down the highway. FEEL the road through your entire body. You are moving slowly and under full control. All of your senses—sight, sound, feeling, smell, taste—are working.

See yourself behind the wheel. Observe how you are dressed.

It is beginning to rain. Notice the raindrops on your windshield. See the shape of the raindrops. Watch their movement as they slide down the window and join each other. The rain on your windshield is all that you are processing. Focus until you can clearly SEE, FEEL, HEAR,

TASTE, AND SMELL the rain. Take a minute and enjoy each one of these sensations: See it—feel it—hear it—taste it—smell it!

You just missed a curve in the road and ran your dream car straight into a telephone pole!

Why did your car hit the telephone pole? Easy, because you did not see where you were going. You were looking in the right direction, but not FOCUSING on the correct distance. It was all a matter of focus.

RELAX. We are going to replay the scene.

You are quiet, calm, and relaxed.

This time only observe the rain.

Your focus is past the windshield and onto the road ahead.

You can still see the rain on your windshield, yet your focus is on the curve and the oncoming telephone pole. You follow the curve in the road and drive safely past the pole. You continue to process the rain on your windshield, but do not focus on it. Experience the difference in focus. You are aware of the rain being there, observing it as a blur, but are not focusing on it. FOCUS is the difference!

Imagery Experience

This experience, and you did have the experience, introduced you to a concept you will be working with throughout this book. This is the use of IMAGERY, ATTENTION, and INTENTION. You will be working with imagery throughout the book, but for right now it is sufficient to say that you DID EXPERIENCE DRIVING THAT CAR. The more passionate your effort with imagery, the greater your result. The more vivid your images, the more powerful your experience.

Take a minute and recall the vividness of your images.

Reflect on the color, sound, feel, and smell of your car. YOU
WERE THERE. That's imagery and focus.

Implementation Triangle

In putting imagery to work for you in sales, it is important to remember that sales is a process, not just a group of
mechanical movements and techniques tied together for
the purpose of moving someone to buy something that they
neither need or want. A sale is one unit. For your work
throughout this book, here is a triangle to assist you in
understanding how the art of sales functions:

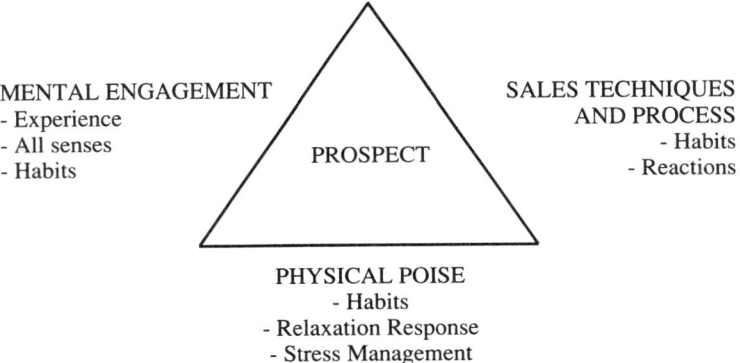

MENTAL ENGAGEMENT
- Experience
- All senses
- Habits

PROSPECT

SALES TECHNIQUES
AND PROCESS
- Habits
- Reactions

PHYSICAL POISE
- Habits
- Relaxation Response
- Stress Management

All elements of your triangle must be present for it to
stand; the same is true for peak performance levels in sales,
you need physical poise, mental engagement, and sales
technique habits. All three elements form one unit, one
motion.

"I repeat: the golf swing can be readily taught,
and consistently performed only if it is conceived
as one motion."
— Ernest Jones, *Swinging The Club*

What Ernest Jones said about the golf swing applies equally to the process of sales, and to the process of learning to sell. Selling can be readily taught and consistently performed only when it is conceived as one "unit." Everything in that unit is a "goes with."

The difficulty with sales training comes with your ability or inability to learn the sales units as one process, one total unit. Keeping in mind that sales is a process, for performance purposes you will be looking at sales as a whole, taking individual parts out, developing and habituating them, and then putting them back into place. The concept of the one "unit" comes first.

The Other Half Of The Sales Lesson — Where Does This Book Fit?

Mark McCormack, Chairman of International Management Group (IMG), is the author of the bestselling book, *What They Don't Teach You At Harvard Business School.* Mark's book represents the other half of training in the business world. It is not the only new business book, but it does represent his opinions and comments on subjects that are not typically presented in business training programs, or at the Harvard Business School. His book can be called the "other half" of business training.

This book could then be said to represent the other half of your sales training. The book's purpose is not to replace other sales books, but to complement them. This is not a book to read, it is a book to do, and you might well find yourself "doing this book" along with another sales book or company sales training program.

Doing This Book

In processing the information in this book, we have found it more effective to read the entire book over lightly the first time. Find out what is in the book, what it is all about and what it is not about, and make friends with it. Then, highlight pertinent information with a yellow highlighter as you read it in-depth the second time. Change colors and add notations in personalizing your focus further in subsequent readings. Reading any book in this manner will enable you to further discover new and powerful information not only about the book, but about yourself as well. One of your objectives can be to become your own marketing expert and sales trainer.

TO MASTER A SKILL, TECHNIQUE, OR EVEN A THOUGHT, it is important to your ultimate success to take one step at a time. It is most effective to stay with one step or technique until that technique is thoroughly yours: inside-out, backward and forward, in your sleep, and habituated. Therefore, upon your second and subsequent readings of this book, you will want to target a technique for implementation and may choose not to read further until that technique or thought is modeled and integrated and becomes yours.

On your initial trip through this book, you can heed two pieces of advice from Ken Blanchard's article, *The One Minute Golfer.*

**ALL GOOD PERFORMANCES
START WITH CLEAR GOALS**

and

**AN ELEPHANT CAN BE EATEN
ONE BITE AT A TIME**

In our sales training programs, we recommend that as you initially read this book you formulate three goals that are a priority to your sales career. Achieve these goals before initiating any others. Accomplish your initial goals, establish additional goals, work to accomplish these, and continue the cycle FOR THE REST OF YOUR LIFE. Remember, life is not a destination, it is a journey.

Before learning more about the mental and technical mechanics of selling and buying, there are some major points we need to review. In learning and re-learning sales skills you can apply the following rules:

- 1. Only commit to habituating a sales technique when you fully understand why it works and why you are implementing it.
- 2. Practice the technique at least 3O repetitions per day for 21 contiguous days. Include mental repetitions in your practice. A habit takes 21 days to develop. Developing effective habits is key to sustained peak levels of performance.
- 3. Give full attention and intention to each act you are doing during practice. Do not practice just to be practicing—have a specific intent. An instructor friend of mine in St. Louis always says that practice does not make perfect; only perfect practice makes perfect.
- 4. Evaluate only the technique you are practicing at that time.
- 5. Separating practice from performance can be a valuable technique. Practice in order to habituate techniques for use in performance and then be sure to put practice and performance back together.
- 6. Make life and learning enjoyable. You are intelligent, and intelligent people continue primarily with that which they enjoy.

Implementation Is The Key

Nothing is over until it is over, and nothing begins until you begin. Nothing magical will happen with the materials between the two covers of this book until you initiate, implement and integrate it into your personal selling style and habit pattern. There must be a beginning and it is yours. The Chinese followers of Tao have a saying that even a journey of a thousand leagues begins but with one step. You have already made a partial commitment by obtaining this book and having read this far. Getting this far is your "one step." It's your beginning. Now, continue on and enjoy the experiences of implementation along the way.

An Implementation Map

So that you can use it as a reference for your journey through this book, here is an implementation process we present in our sales seminars. There are six major steps:

```
Discovery < - - - - - < - - - - - < - - - - - < - - - - - |
   v                                         ^
Discomfort
   v                                         |
Understanding                                ^
(concept)                       Continual Feedback
   v                                  Loop
Practice/Drill/Rehearse                      |
(Skills)                                     ^
   v                                         |
Implementation                               ^
   v                                         |
Integration                                  ^
   v
CREATIVITY > - - - - - > - - - - - > - - - - - > - - - |
```

This is a learning and implementation map you can use throughout this book. Creativity, the last step, is what your selling will be all about at the more advanced levels of peak performance, because EFFECTIVE SELLING IS CREATIVE SELLING.

You may want to take just a second and think about that last statement: "Effective selling is creative selling."

- 1. DISCOVERY. You discover a new and different technique, piece of knowledge, or idea that has potential for the development of your ability to help more people.
- 2. A sense of DISCOMFORT. Research has shown that some sense of discomfort or need must follow discovery if any action is to occur. When everything is fine the way it is, then there is no reason to change, and you won't. Have you heard the saying, "If it ain't broke, don't fix it"? This is where self-motivation comes in. By definition, motivation is the inward desire to fulfill an unmet drive, need, or want. Once a particular drive is met, it is no longer as intense a motivator in that situation. YOU must provide the personal drive to energize your actions. Yours is the fuel that fires the development process.
- 3. UNDERSTANDING. To become effective, what you are attempting to learn must begin to make some kind of sense to you. Not to me, but to you. Your mind is constantly working to integrate new discoveries with what you already know. Do not worry, your brain will either make some sense of the information, consciously or unconsciously, or reject it. Throughout this book we will not always be talking about the kind of sense where one plus one always equals two. Sometimes ONE plus ONE will equal BLUE. Do not worry, your mind knows what it is processing and how it is processing it.

- 4. PRACTICE/DRILL/REHEARSE. You develop an image of how the technique or idea will function in reality. This is vital to the total process. You learn to picture it (whatever "it" is) working first on the walls of your mind. This is mental imagery (also called "visualization") and you will be devoting a lot of time and practice to it later. You will be working at the conscious level of skill development. A technique or idea needs a way to manifest itself. It is great to have an image in your mind, but until you make the connections through the neuropathways of your body and mind, little outward action or behavior can result. This practice can be in the form of role play, use of video tape, or other training techniques. We recommend that this initial level of implementation occur WITHOUT a prospect present. This is the practice, drill, and rehearsal part of your training. You will learn how to separate practice from performance, and then put them back together again, a technique far too few of us master.
- 5. IMPLEMENTATION. DO IT NOW! Isolate one technique as you work through this book; then work on that specific item and prepare to add it to your sales calls. Invest thirty days towards developing the technique into a habit.
- 6. INTEGRATION. When integration occurs, you are functioning more at the habitual level. The new behavior becomes yours. It becomes a part of you. It is you and you are it. This is not something you can force. Like sleep, integration comes naturally and becomes part of you naturally. You prepare through the previous five steps of the process and then "allow" it to happen.
- 7. CREATIVITY. Now that you have it, go out and create with it. As they say on *StarTrek*, "Go where no

man has gone before." Creativity is what supports your performance at peak levels in sales.

Implementation Log

To support your implementation of the techniques presented throughout the book, areas of workspace have been provided in the appropriate sections. This space will become your personal log. Construct your own implementation manual within the sections provided. This book is your guide to the other side of sales performance, so write in it, change it, create it, add to it, make it yours.

Separate Practice From Performance

Arnold Palmer does not see a new golf technique, then immediately go out and "try" it in the next golf tournament. He has an implementation plan. People new to sales, and even us oldtimers, also require quality time to habituate new skills before calling on prospects. You need your own implementation strategy.

Surgeons do not "try" to open up a live patient the first time they have a knife in their hands. Race car drivers do not "try" new steering techniques in the Indy 5OO Race. And none of the golf pros who have consulted with us wait until the PGA Tournament to "try" a new swing technique. Golf legend Sam Snead is said to have been watching a young tournament player on the practice tee just before a tournament was to begin. It must have been obvious to Sam that the young man was attempting to develop a new shot, or working on a technique someone had just shown him. Sam then gave that young player the best advice he could have, and it fits your selling skills as well. He told him that "if he hadn't brought it to the course with him he wasn't going to find it there."

In sales, when you fail to take an "habituated" sales technique on the sales call with you, don't attempt to find it in front of the prospect. When you practice in front of the prospect, all four of you lose—you, your company, the technique, and most of all, the prospect!

Supporting you in the development of sales skills BEFORE you make the call, and therefore being able to take appropriate sales skills with you, is one objective of this book.

Enjoy The Journey Through Your Book

2

He Walked Into The Client's Closet and Would Not Come Out

Preparing Yourself For The Sale

Terry knew the banking industry inside and out, had done well in all of the company's sales training programs, and knew the product better than most of the salespeople who had been with the company for a much longer period of time. Yet his first sales call was a total disaster and he actually ended up walking right into the prospect's closet and would not come out! He was just that nervous and unprepared mentally. And as a mind reader I can also answer your question; yes, he left the field of selling.

Terry had gone on the sales call well prepared, or so all of us in the office thought. He was making a call on a customer who was already using our firm's products and services, yet he got so nervous that he actually walked into the prospect's closet and would not come out for several minutes.

You may not have made the mistake of walking into a client's closet, but have you ever "choked" before a prospect or a group? If you have, then you know it is an experience you do not want to repeat. When you choke on a sales call, or when an athlete "chokes" on the field of competition, as so many of us have, please understand that the word choke becomes a literal term. This is because the brain is somewhat mechanistic and understands only in literal terms—it then signals the body to follow these messages. Some salespeople and athletes actually become so nervous that they actually cut off their own air supply, stop breathing, and literally choke.

What was missing from Terry's sales skills was poise, or relaxation. In NLP technology, this is called a "resource state," a state when you are able to make behavioral choices with ease. Our "closet salesperson" lacked both poise and a relaxation response to stress, and as a result he walked right "into the closet," right into a state of high anxiety. What Terry had done was to overdevelop his stress response and not develop an appropriate relaxation response. His relaxation response to pressure was missing—and few salespeople see it as a skill or habit that can be learned and used on a regular basis. To sell effectively, relaxation and poise are a must. They are part of your foundation for success. Please recall that Chapter 1 presented a relaxation response as the foundation of your sales triangle.

Relax First

When learning any of the sales techniques in this book, it is recommended that you go through a general relaxation exercise first. Make this type of exercise a habit. At first the relaxation process can seem mechanical, but you will anchor it very quickly. You will notice yourself getting more and more relaxed as your skill level develops. Once you feel yourself achieve a relaxed state, you can turn your attention to the actual activity or technique you are learning. When you are tense, your progress will be slow and difficult at best.

For your own selling, think of physical poise and relaxation states metaphorically as the oil that allows you to function successfully. The oil in your car does not run the car; it ALLOWS it to function freely. Physical poise, or a relaxed state of mind and body, is the oil for your selling. The objective for this section is for you to be able to raise your level of poise and relaxation at will, especially during your conscious selling hours.

As you go through the relaxation exercise we are presenting, it is important for you to use a tape recording of the technique and associated drill. You can:

1. Use an existing imagery tape. These tapes are listed in the Reference Section at the back of the book.
2. Record the following exercise yourself.
3. Have someone read the exercise to you the first few times you go through it and until you are familiar with the process.

Your objective for the drill is relaxation, not sleep. It is important to remember, however, that what happens is just that—what happens. Should you go to sleep, then you went to sleep. Have a nice trip. Be easy on yourself. Your body was telling you that you needed the rest. However, do not make it a practice to fall asleep during any relaxation or imagery drill.

We had one salesperson who used this technique lying down and never made it through the first two minutes before going into very slow brain wave patterns, called sleep. She finally had to use the technique sitting up to get its full advantage. You will want to develop your own implementation style as well.

General Relaxation Technique

(Please follow these instructions)
- Go into a quiet place. Your place.
- Lie down or sit in a comfortable position.
- Remove, or loosen, any items that bind you.
- Close your eyes.
- Turn your thoughts to your breathing. Breathe deeply. Take air in through your nose and exhale through your mouth. Let your stomach move out freely. Completely fill your lungs with air. Fill them from the bottom up.
- Synchronize your breathing with your heartbeats. Relax and feel your heartbeat. Do this now. Breathe in slowly through your nose for six heartbeats.
- Inhale the air deep into the bottom of your lungs. Your shoulders and neck are relaxed.
- Exhale through your mouth for six beats.
- Relax and begin the cycle again.
- Relax. Breathe in six . . . out six . . . in six . . . continue the cycle.
- Imagine inhaling a white mist that cleanses your lungs. It permeates your lung walls and travels through your body. Let its vibrancy swirl through areas that are tense. Expel all tension and discomfort as you exhale.
- Let your body relax deeply. Deeper than ever before.
- Give attention to images as they appear. Images are how you think. Images are you.
- Notice the colors you see. Notice the textures you feel. Notice the smell of the air around you and the sounds you hear.
- You are calm and sensing tastes.
- You are quiet and feel light.
- Relax and let go of any tension.

- Allow your mind to wander. Continue breathing deeply and freely. In for six . . . out for six.
- Relax and feel the vibrancy travel through your body. It is in your muscles, now in your bones, now in your blood stream.
- You can do anything. You can be anywhere.
- There is no need to make things happen. They happen naturally.
- Relax. Know that your images are always there.
- Listen, notice, and enjoy. Continue to breathe freely and relax.

A Few More Basics

As you advance through your relaxation exercise there are a few habits you will want to ensure that you develop effectively. One is breathing. Believe it or not, most of the people who come to us for training have forgotten how to breathe effectively. This includes athletes as well as salespeople. While working with a swim team in Florida, we discovered that close to 60% of the swimmers needed to improve their breathing techniques. You would assume that swimmers, of all athletes, would have developed outstanding control of their breathing. This is a false assumption, as are most assumptions.

When you become nervous on a sales call, breathing is the first thing that you restrict. You actually begin to "choke."

To Do

To check your breathing right now, first lie down in a comfortable position. Place one hand near the bottom of your stomach, the other on the top of your chest. As you breathe in, you begin filling your lungs from the bottom, not the top. As you do the following drill, the hand on your stomach should move up before the hand on your chest. You will find that the hand on your chest actually moves very little. This form of deep breathing will build both lung capacity and your ability to relax. Oxygen is a supporter of life, and you need more oxygen for your relaxation response to pressure.

Next, re-discover how to feel your heart beating through your body. You will be timing your breathing cycle around the beating of your heart. Should sensing your heart through your body not be normal for you right now, do not worry. Years ago, you had the sensation of your heart beating throughout your body; you just got distracted and lost the feeling someplace along the way. You will re-establish the feeling.

* Now, please breathe in for six beats, out for six beats, in for six, and then repeat the cycle. Repeat the cycle for one minute.

Should you still not be able to feel your heart beating through your body, do the following. The next time you use your relaxation routine, get into counting your breathing cycle. Begin to relax, and then locate your pulse with your hand. Take the two forefingers on your right hand, locate your jugular vein in the middle of the left side of your neck with these two fingers, and feel your pulse. Pattern the timing of your breathing to your pulse. Now relax and identify your pulse throughout the remainder of your body. As with every technique in this book, DO NOT FORCE IT. ALLOW THE FEELING TO DEVELOP. It may take several days to re-establish the feeling, but it is there. You will find it.

Before long you will be able to feel your pulse without using your two fingers.

Peeling Your Orange

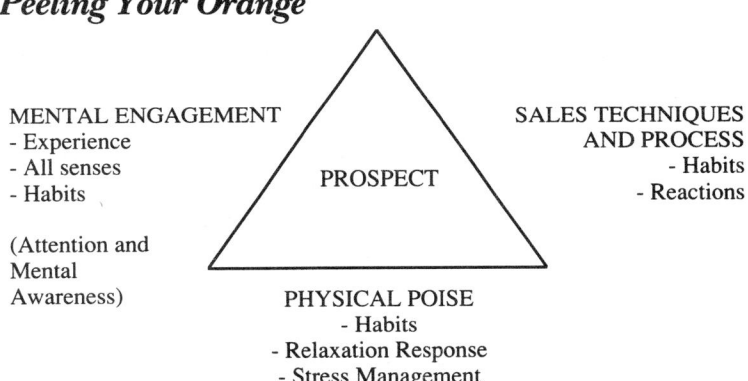

MENTAL ENGAGEMENT
- Experience
- All senses
- Habits

(Attention and
Mental
Awareness)

PROSPECT

SALES TECHNIQUES
AND PROCESS
- Habits
- Reactions

PHYSICAL POISE
- Habits
- Relaxation Response
- Stress Management

Mental awareness or attention is the second element necessary for you to perform at peak levels in sales. You have been introduced to the physical poise or relaxation side of the triangle, so let's move on to the passionate side, mental engagement.

NOTE: You can begin to habituate your relaxation response and breathing awareness by placing them on a 21-day plan and still continue through the book. However, remember to keep your relaxation response and breathing awareness on schedule.

The following technique was designed to involve and intensify all of your sensory modes and assist you in creating a higher sense of mental awareness. As with the previous exercise, get someone to read the drill to you when possible. Or, if you prefer, read it into a tape recorder.

- Go into a quiet place. Your place.
- Close your eyes.
- Go through your deep breathing exercise. In for six

. . . out for six . . . continue with the cycle.
- Hear the sound of your breath.
- Feel your heartbeat throughout your entire body.
- Visualize going to the refrigerator. Open the door. Feel the cold air flow out, down, and around your feet.
- See your orange inside the refrigerator. Notice its size, shape, and texture. Notice where it is sitting. What else do you see in the refrigerator? Smell?
- Put your hand inside and pick out the orange. Bring it back out. Roll the orange around in your palms. Feel its size, weight, shape, and texture. Allow it to rest in your palms for a moment. Go over to the table.
- Slowly dig your fingers into the peel and begin removing it. Feel the peeling under your fingernails. Feel the resistance of the skin as you peel it back from the fruit. Feel the juice on your hand. Lay the peelings on the table.
- Peel the orange entirely. Hear the sound. Notice the smell. Allow some of the juice to run down the back of your hand and down your arm.
- Allow the orange to rest in your palms for a moment.
- Smell your orange. Bring it closer to your nose. Now smell it again.
- Break the orange into halves and set one-half on the table. Now quarters. Finally, into sections.
- With all of your senses, examine that section. Bring it close to your nose and smell it. Now bite the section in half. Taste it. Feel the juice in your mouth, on your tongue, and now going down your throat.
- Eat the remaining half of the section.
- Take a napkin from the table and dry your hands and lips.

- Examine this experience as long as you wish before re-opening your eyes.
- Most of all, enjoy. HAVE FUN!

Record Your Responses

Now that you have completed the exercise, record your responses to the following questions. The act of writing serves to reinforce your experiences.

How did the experience make you FEEL (both physically and emotionally)?

_____

_____

_____

_____

What senses did you use?

_____

_____

_____

_____

Describe your feeling of relaxation.

_____

_____

_____

_____

How much did you enjoy the orange?

_____

_____

_____

_____

You can continue using the "peeling your orange" exercise as a method of further developing your awareness skills.

Imagery

The technique you used in tasting your orange, AND YOU DID TASTE IT, was imagery. Imagery will become increasingly important to the development of your sales career and to the effective utilization of the techniques in this book. Observers of past Olympics have already seen the transformation to imagery training and performance by top performers. Athletes competing in the Olympic Biathlon knew all about being mentally aware and physically poised. Their task in the Biathlon was to mentally see a calm heartbeat after strenuous physical exercise. In the Biathlon, participants snow skied cross-country for several miles and then had to stop and shoot at seven small targets with a rifle. Imagery skills helped them develop control over their bodily processes and instantly slow down their racing heartbeats. Their strategy in this event was to physically excel in the skiing, stop, slow down their heartbeat, and fire at the targets in time with their heartbeats. Sound difficult? It was, and it was not "natural." Biathlon participants trained their minds to perform and then their minds trained their bodies. That is right, their bodies were trained by their minds, not the other way around.

In performing at peak levels in sales, realizing that your mind trains your body through imagery is key to your success. This is one of the most difficult lessons for both salespeople and athletes to learn—the mind trains the body, the body does not train the mind.

Picking Up Your Pizza

While you are all warmed up, let's do another imagery drill to reinforce your understanding of how your mind programs your body through imagery.

- Mentally get into your car so that you can drive over and pick up a pizza at your favorite location.
- You are in your car, have been driving, and now need to make a turn into the parking lot of the place where you will get your pizza. Before you begin to slow the speed of your car and turn the wheel, you have already formed the specific image of the turn you are about to make. In your mind you already have the image of making that turn. Your body understands the process very well and responds to the images habitually.
- You finish the turn, pick up your pizza, and drive home safely because of the images you process habitually and unconsciously, without giving them a second thought.

Do not forget that images are not limited to seeing, or visualization. This is a very important distinction. Here are two words, APPLE PIE. These may be just words, but what image do they create in your mind's eye? Close your eyes and mentally look at that apple pie. Is the pie hot or cold? That's OK, take a minute and find out.

Is the pie plain or have you covered it with ice cream? How does your hot pie SMELL? How does the crust FEEL to your touch? What do you associate with it? Your family? Holidays? Go ahead, touch it.

Is your mouth watering yet?

Take some time just to process your images and enjoy your apple pie, you deserve the rest and relaxation.

Separating Practice From Performance

Imagery skills allow you to separate practice from performance while you are learning, re-learning, and rehearsing sales techniques. When all of your sensory rheostats are turned to high, and your images are intense and active, you ARE practicing, you ARE performing. The images are real. The images are you. Through vivid imagery, sales situations become real. Prospects are there. This powerful form of practice has the same effect on your ability to perform as if you were with that prospect in their office. But then through effective imagery, you *are* in their office.

Peter Jacobsen (golf touring professional) was playing in a golf tournament and preparing to play an iron shot onto the green. He took the golf club from Mike, his caddie, walked over to the golf ball, stood over it for a minute or two, took a couple of practice swings, walked back over to Mike, handed him the club, and walked off. Mike stood still for an instant in utter disbelief. Peter had walked away WITHOUT HITTING THE BALL. Peter's mental imagery in preparation for the shot had been so strong, his images so vivid, that to him he had already hit the shot. In fact, his body made every single action and reaction just as if he had hit the shot. HE HAD HIT THE BALL! That was great preparation and at that point in time he was performing on the other side. And yes, he did go back and hit the ball!

All of the professionals with whom we work, including you, know that two of the keys to effective practice are vivid imagery and relaxation.

Prove It!

I can hear you saying to yourself, "Prove it! Prove to me that being mentally aware through imagery and physically poised through relaxation will support my becoming more effective in sales!"

One vital lesson to learn in sales is that you do not prove anything to prospects. That is correct; prospects prove things to themselves, you only assist in the process. So, take a minute and prove the concepts of imagery and relaxation to yourself. You will need a few supplies for the exercise so please get them now. You will need:

1. A piece of string about fourteen inches long.

2. An object to tie on to the end of the string. A car key will work nicely.

3. And a flat surface. Your desk will do.

4. Place your elbow on the table (refer to the example below), bend your wrist slightly, and hold the string that the key almost touches the table. Your eyes are open and focused on the key hanging at the end of the string. You are calm, quiet, and relaxed.

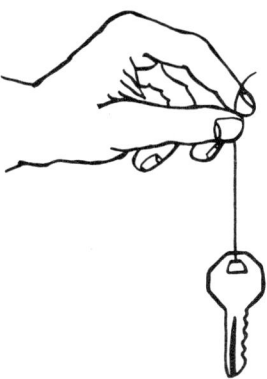

1. Do not consciously move the string with your hand. Keep your eyes open and begin to image the key swinging right and then left. See it moving only slightly at first. See the key swinging right and left. It is swinging further right and now further left. Relax, let it happen. Your image is

working for you.

2. Imagine the key stopped. Allow the key time to stop swinging.

3. Look at the key as it moves away from you and then back toward you, moving only slightly at first, away from you and now back toward you.

4. Your arm and hand are calm, quiet, and relaxed. Image the key's movements.

5. Experiment on your own for a few minutes. The key will respond to your images. Move it in circles. Play with it, have fun. You are quiet, calm, and relaxed. Should you not have gotten a clear visual image on this drill, remember that imagery is a skill and your skills may need additional development.

TIGHTEN YOUR MUSCLES.

6. With the key centered and not moving, tighten your hand, your wrist, and now your arm. That's it, tighter.

7. With your muscles remaining tight, imagine the key moving to your right and then left. Slightly right and then left. It is not working!

8. THERE IS LITTLE OR NO MOVEMENT. Tighten your hand more and work harder. Imagine the key moving then slightly left. This is not going to work. What happened?

Why Did The Key Swing In The First Example?

"Physically relaxed" AND "Mentally aware through imagery" will move the key. Mentally aware and physically tense will NOT allow you to move the key as well. Mentally asleep and physically tense will not work either. The reason your images moved the key in the first example is because YOUR MIND AND BODY ARE ONE UNIT.

When you form an image in your mind, your body will

do everything it can to complete that image, and it does so in direct proportion to the strength of that image. As you anticipated the key moving to the right, your mind created the image, you saw it happening, and your body, cued by the signals from your brain, reacted to the image. To your body, the key was already moving. The result? Your body reacted to the image and the key moved. The movement was slight, and it took the key at the end of the string to detect it, but the movement was there.

The same is true of your new techniques for sales training. You can make sales calls in the theater of your mind, and your body will respond as if you were actually making the call. The call you image is the call you get. Remember, your mind and body are one unit.

Being physically poised and in a resourceful state through a relaxation response is the other half of the formula in moving the key. When you tightened your arm in the second example, the nerve impulses from your brain, stimulated by the image, could not fire down to the muscle. Your muscles were already firing and in a tense position. When physically relaxed, your body can respond to the images created in your mental training. When physically tense, your body does not have the chance to respond because the messages do not get through.

"Mentally aware" and "Physically relaxed" is the formula for success. There was a time not very long ago when this formula was considered to be "abnormal" for salespeople and that you had to be "up" to sell.

New age science is suggesting that you are not only affecting a subject with thought, but that you cannot even consider a subject without having an effect on it. It is your choice—what effect do you want?

Rules of Imagery

In re-establishing your ability to use imagery as a productive learning, development, and implementation tool for sales, here are a few rules:

- 1. GIVE YOURSELF TIME. Give yourself the opportunity to grow within this new approach to sales. Do not expect to be a Picasso when you have just bought your first set of watercolors. Your images will grow in color, strength, brightness, and closeness to you the more you practice. You will also be able to consciously manipulate your images and change their elements, or "submodalities." These are the finer differences in your sensory systems (when you visualize an apple, it can be within a black and white photograph or in a color movie). These distinctions are created using "submodalities."
- 2. DO NOT "TRY." ALLOW IMAGES TO HAPPEN. Whenever you try, it is a sure sign that you are "disassociated," or *outside* the activity looking in. You are separated from the experience by "trying" to get into it. You are better off to "intuit." Our formal sales training program includes several relaxation tapes. The objective of using the tapes is to help participants foster internal development and work from an "associated state" of mind (*inside* themselves). When you get "intuit," you are no longer "trying." Think of the stress that is associated with the word "trying." What happens when you try to go to sleep? What happens when you try to make yourself relax? Do not try; do!
- 3. IMAGES THAT OCCUR ARE APPROPRIATE FOR YOU AT THE TIME. Your images are not good, not bad; they just are. Resist the temptation to judge your images. Merely observe and enjoy

them. If you go to sleep during relaxation sessions, then you must have needed it.

- 4. PRACTICE IS KEY. The more you commit to image and relaxation practice, the greater the power it will have in your life and sales career. Tests with imagery prove its effectiveness even in contributing to well-being in the treatment of illnesses. One of the reasons for its success with people who are ill is that they really have a perceived need for it. When faced with loss of health, people make a commitment. Sales is not a life or death situation, even though some people make it that way. Even so, your images are the life of your sales. Commit to them now!

- 5. ENJOY WORKING WITH IMAGERY. When you enjoy a task, you have a tendency to stay with it longer and work more effectively.

- 6. BE KIND TO YOURSELF. This is the last rule, but first among them in importance.

Use Imagery With Goal Setting

NLP technology includes a process called an "ecology check." This is when you check with all the inner parts of yourself and make sure that each part is in agreement/rapport with your ultimate goal. This can help you move forward smoothly toward your desired result.

When setting goals, use your imagery techniques to create the RESULTS associated with each goal and check out if those are the actual goals you are after. Remember that you do not DO A GOAL; you do specific tasks and activities that take you towards the achievement of your goal.

Begin By Being Kind To Yourself.
You Are It!

3

You Can Judge a Building's Height by the Depth of Its Foundation

Preparation Before The Sale

The Gateway Arch to the West stands over 600 feet tall in St. Louis, Missouri. You can visit the monument, ride to the top, and have a beautiful view of St. Louis. There's no lunch at the top, just a great view. On your trip to the Arch be sure to take time out to see the movie on its conception, design, and construction. During the movie, pay particular attention to the depth and work on the foundation for the Arch and you will learn a valuable lesson for sales.

People who were in St. Louis to see the work on the foundation for the Arch are not surprised to see the height of the finished structure. Those of us who witnessed the construction of the Arch know that without the proper foundation, this great monument could not withstand the conditions it must face. The same is true for your sales career. Your rise to success will occur in direct proportion to the construction of your foundation.

The third element of your performance triangle is "sales techniques." As much as possible, the integration of

your sales techniques needs to be done before your actual
sales call.

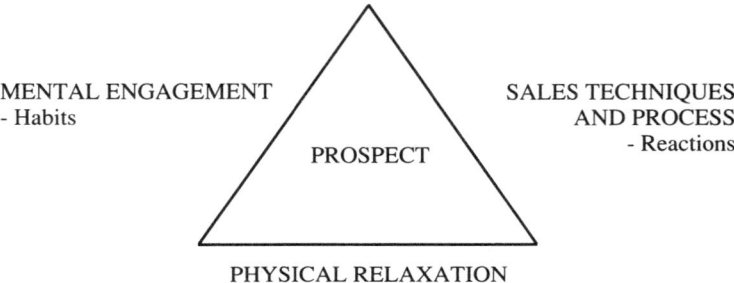

MENTAL ENGAGEMENT   SALES TECHNIQUES
- Habits   AND PROCESS
                    PROSPECT   - Reactions

PHYSICAL RELAXATION

Travel back to St. Louis, Missouri for a moment. Most
of the people viewing the Arch are not aware of the work
that went into forming its foundation. All they see is the
finished product, the Arch. Foundations are, for the most
part, unseen and unappreciated by the casual observer. Yet,
without the foundation the finished product could not
stand. The same is true for your sales career.

THE HEIGHT OF YOUR SUCCESS
WILL OCCUR IN DIRECT PROPORTION
TO THE DEPTH
OF YOUR PREPARATION

The value of your preparation may not be recognized
by those around you and may even be discouraged by some.
One of my early sales managers did not want to see us in
the office preparing. Bill saw our jobs as getting out and
selling, not preparing! As a sales manager, Bill must have
seen his job as getting us out of the office and keeping us
out, and not as preparing us to sell more effectively. Believ-
ing the "big lie" of spending all of your time selling and not
investing any of that time in preparation never got anyone

selling at peak levels in major accounts.

What is important is that YOU know and appreciate your foundation, your preparation for sales. Prospects will not see or appreciate your preparation, but they can appreciate your preparation through the problems you solve for them. Not even your manager will see all of your preparation. You are the only one who can appreciate fully the contribution preparation makes to your success in sales. You will always know!

You Can Ask Too Many Questions

Individuals new to the profession of sales have a tendency to gather their initial account information from the prospect, and not from other forms of research and preparation BEFORE the sales call. While it is true that prospects enjoy talking about their own organizations, products and services, and even some of their business problems, they do NOT enjoy the task of educating new salespeople. Asking too many questions at this stage of the sale can stop the cycle.

Use initial calls to verify information that you have gathered during research and you will be much more effective in helping prospects.

Also consider the level of the individual you are asking questions of. Questions that are appropriate at entry level positions within an organization are typically not appropriate for the CEO. Design your questions to match both the individual and the situation.

Enthusiasm

Yes, you can prepare for enthusiasm! Of all the words

used in the field of sales, enthusiasm is perhaps the least understood and most abused by managers and salespeople alike. One popular sales book states that:

> If you have enthusiasm
> and love your work,
> you will work hard.

Give yourself a minute and think about what that quote is really saying to you. Then ask yourself, "Is the statement true?"

If you believe the quotation ("If you have enthusiasm and love your work, you will work hard."), you should have a question, because there are elements missing. If someone told you that when you were enthusiastic and loved weight-lifting you would have a lot of muscles, would you believe them? No, because there is a missing element.

What if someone told you that if you were enthusiastic and loved making presentations you would have a lot of success with presentations? Would you believe them? Certainly not, because again there is a missing element. Enthusiasm is important to the sales process but we need to begin by talking about what produces enthusiasm, and which elements in the process come first.

The statement, "If you have enthusiasm and love your work you will work hard" may be pointing you in the wrong direction. You conceptually understand your work, develop an appreciation and respect for it, and actually "work" before you develop a true love and appreciation for that work or vocation. The word enthusiasm is formed from two Greek words meaning "God within." Enthusiasm then, by definition, develops from within. You are the one responsible for creating your own enthusiasm. Can outside forces help create and support your enthusiasm? Certainly they can, but the primary responsibility remains with the individual.

Since enthusiasm has to be created from within you, the next question is "what do you create it from?" There must be ingredients available to create that enthusiasm. The remainder of this chapter presents two major ingredients of enthusiasm: product knowledge and a working knowledge of people.

Learn How Your Product Is Being Used

During a sales seminar we were conducting in Kentucky for a company marketing retirement communities, one of the participants who was new to the field of sales was having a difficult time grasping some of the sales concepts and techniques being presented. By the end of the first morning it became obvious that Amanda (not her real name) was not struggling with the sales techniques as much as with her lack of product knowledge. It was unrealistic to ask Amanda to be ENTHUSIASTIC about learning techniques to sell something she neither understood nor believed in. Got the image?

We asked the director of marketing to set up an interview for the next morning with one of the couples in the retirement center where we were doing the training. Nothing was to be guided, planned, or rehearsed. We wanted their candid reaction to one major question, "Why retire here?" What we got the next day could never have been planned or staged—it was too good.

Mr. and Mrs. Williams were in their eighties. The Williams' had lived all of their married lives on their farm and had been in the retirement center for about a year. What they told the group had very little to do with retirement and everything to do with LIVING. In describing "why retire here," the Williams' talked of security, health, and perhaps most of all, self-respect. What was to be a fifteen minute interview turned into two sessions of over an hour each. The company video taped the second interview with the couple for ALL employees, not just salespeople, to see. Better than any product manual or blueprint for construction, the Williams' defined the essence of what that retirement center was really offering. The center was not selling medical care, food, shelter, or most of the features they thought they were selling. That sales staff was selling the miracle their center performed for people just like the Williams'. What the staff of that retirement center was selling was LIFE ITSELF.

Before you even think of discounting the importance of selling a more abundant life, consider traveling to that retirement center in Louisville and talking with the residents who once saw retirement as death and learn from them about their new and enriched lives.

After those interviews, the participants in our sales seminar had little doubt concerning what they were really selling. Now the participants actually had individual images of what they were selling. Their images were of the people they were serving and of the dignity that retirement centers could provide. Most important of all, the smiles on the faces of Mr. and Mrs. Williams were etched forever on the walls of their minds.

Amanda learned a great deal that day about enthusiasm from the very clients she was serving. And yes, Amanda began to model the sales skills with greater ease.

Become A Business Problem Solver

A month after one of our sales training programs, we received a call from Judy, a program participant. She called to tell us that she was making progress on her three goals from the program but that she had found a new source of enthusiasm for her selling. Her next words were, "Why didn't you tell us that we are not salespeople at all, but really business problem solvers!"

Judy was very close to being right on target, but there are multiple sides to that coin. Yes, you are a business problem solver, but effective selling calls for a win-win-win situation. The prospect wins through your help in solving their business problems, but both you and your organization need to benefit as well if there is to be a long-term business relationship.

Product Assignment

Here is your second assignment in product knowledge and experience. Learn what problems your offering can solve by listening to, not talking at, the customers who own and use your products and services. Learn what problems your offering can solve by listening to, not talking at, the customers who own and use your products and services. That is not a printing error; some things are just worth writing out twice.

PRODUCT KNOWLEDGE IS VASTLY DIFFERENT FROM PRODUCT EXPERIENCE. A great number of salespeople have product knowledge, but fewer have product experience. One way to effectively gain product experience, and form the images you need for selling, is to go out and visit your existing customers. As you talk with customers, watch their faces, remember them, and form images through their experiences with your offerings. Listen carefully to their stories, and you will form the images to fuel the enthusiasm you need to develop your own success in sales.

The Negative Things

Do not be afraid of hearing negative comments about your offerings. No product is perfect. In the balance, however, YOU MUST VOTE FOR YOUR PRODUCT, not against it, before you can ever begin to represent your company and its offerings to others. How do you vote right now for:

YOUR COMPANY?
YOUR FACILITIES?
YOUR PRODUCTS AND SERVICES?
YOUR SERVICE AFTER THE SALE?
YOUR OWN ABILITY TO HELP PROSPECTS
AND CUSTOMERS?
YOUR CUSTOMERS?

Definition Of "Product"

The definitions you use are important; they are the labels which reflect your unique model of "reality." In this book, we are defining "product" as a set of tangible and intangible attributes, including packaging, pricing, storage distribution, promotion, prestige, and related services, which buyers accept as satisfying both their needs and wants. In the space below, define your product offerings.

_____

_____

_____

_____

_____

_____

_____

How Much Must I Know About My Product?

Your motto for this area of preparation should be, "I can never know too much about my product offering, service, and company, but I can talk too much about them." BALANCE is important in all areas of life, is absolutely essential in sales, and includes the area of product knowledge. What individuals know the most about life insurance? Probably the actuaries. That does not mean they would make the most effective salespeople. What individuals in a car dealership know the most about how automobiles operate? Probably the mechanics. That does not mean they would make the most effective salespeople. Product knowledge is important, but keep it in perspective, in balance.

The point here is that while product knowledge is a must, it is only effective when combined with a working knowledge of people and sales skills. Product knowledge is another "goes with."

Some Questions For You

Here are some product related questions you can research and answer for yourself *before* you begin to sell.

1. WHEN PROSPECTS MAKE A DECISION IN FAVOR OF MY PRODUCTS, WHAT DRIVES DO THOSE PRODUCTS ACTUALLY FULFILL FOR THEM? WHAT PART OF THE PRODUCT AM I? WHAT PART OF THE PRODUCT IS MY COMPANY? Note: When you want to sell more effectively, focus on needs, wants, and beliefs with respect to the *problems* of individual prospects and their organizations instead of needs, wants, beliefs, and problems of you and your organiza-

tion. Customer statistics are a low priority here. Individual prospect concerns are what count most in this situation.
YOUR RESPONSE:

_____

_____

_____

_____

_____

_____

2. WHAT SPECIFIC BUSINESS PROBLEMS IS MY PRODUCT DESIGNED TO SOLVE? AND WHAT ADDITIONAL BUSINESS PROBLEMS AM I TRAINED TO SOLVE?
YOUR RESPONSE:

_____

_____

_____

_____

_____

_____

3. WHAT MAKES MY PRODUCT OFFERING BETTER THAN MY COMPETITION'S? Note: The more specific you get in answering this question the more effective you can become in sales. Your answers respond to feelings, facts, and figures—all of which revolve around features of your products. Omit speculations and opinions; determine the facts. Your company, and its name and reputation, is part of your total product, so be certain to do your homework on how people think about your company.
YOUR RESPONSE:

_____

_____

_____
_____
_____
_____

4. WHO SAYS MY PRODUCTS ARE BETTER? AND, SO WHAT? Note: Here is where personal testimonies and user satisfaction are reported. This is not the place for abstract statements. Concrete application stories are what you are looking for—proof for what others say, not from what you or your company says or thinks.
YOUR RESPONSE:

_____
_____
_____
_____
_____
_____

5. WHAT IS MY PRODUCT, REALLY? Now is the time to define your products in terms of benefits received, problems solved or avoided, and needs, wants, and beliefs met. This is not a features presentation. We talk more about benefits and features in Chapter 8, but air conditioning in your car is only a feature until you use it. One benefit of air conditioning is that you can drive to your sales calls in the middle of summer, when it is humid and 90 degrees by early morning, and not sweat through that new suit of yours. Determine potential benefits here, not features.
YOUR RESPONSE:

_____
_____
_____
_____
_____

6. WHY SHOULD PROSPECTS DECIDE IN MY FAVOR? Unless prospects find themselves with an order taker, they typically do not purchase from a company, they purchase from another individual. Research shows that prospects usually turn into customers and do business with people they like. Why should prospects do business with someone they dislike? Remember, when prospect emotion and prospect logic begin their initial debate, emotion is likely to win out.
YOUR RESPONSE:

_____
_____
_____
_____
_____
_____

7. WHY SHOULD PROSPECTS BUY RIGHT NOW? Prospects typically are saying something to themselves like, "We have lived this long without your product, why do we need it right now? You are not going out of business are you?" This has everything to do with a prospect's priorities, time schedule, rapport with you, and the perceived value of your offering. You had better find out early in the sales process where your prospects are on these points. There are times when, in order to assist the prospect, you will become involved in helping them review their priorities and time schedules.
YOUR RESPONSE:

_____
_____
_____
_____
_____

These are questions you need to answer and EX-

PERIENCE for yourself. Make no mistake; this will require a good deal of work on your part. But it is work that only you can experience for yourself. As you research and answer these questions do not rely on memory. Record your responses in your log. Make this an ongoing process. Become a student of your total product.

Learning About Your Prospect's Business

When working in a foreign country, it seems obvious that the more you learn about its language, customs, and priorities, the easier business is to transact. Remember one thing: YOU ARE ALWAYS A FOREIGNER IN YOUR PROSPECT'S OFFICE. That is neither good nor bad, it just is. And unless you quit your company and join theirs, you will never be an inside part of their organization. You can be useful to their organization, yet you will always remain outside, not a native. As an outsider, prospects do not care about your language, your customs, or the conditions of your business. What they care everything about is their environment, their business.

Most salespeople read their organization's publications, subscribe to at least one magazine on sales or business, know most of the terms connected with their offering and the prices, and possess a reasonable understanding of the major applications their particular offering fulfills. What many of these same salespeople are lacking is a working knowledge of their prospect's . . .

Business language
Industry publications
Trends and issues
General environment and conditions

A Final Remark

When you make calls on prospects, the more work you do in preparation, the less time you will need to invest in creating interest (fact-finding) once you are with them. You still need to verify information you have obtained, and get prospects talking early in the sales call, but effective preparation does save you valuable customer selling time. And more important to the prospect, it saves them valuable work time.

When prospects come into your location cold (hopefully they are close to 98.6 degrees) YOU STILL HAVE PREPARATION BEFORE THE SALE. When you begin to think that the only reason people walk through your door is because it is unlocked, your sales process is in real trouble. Success in sales requires that you find out as much about your CUSTOMER BASE as possible.

"The harder you work, the luckier you get."
—Gary Player, Touring Golf Professional

4

Salespeople Are Not Lizards, However . . .

Personal Preparation Before The Sale

Great salespeople we have worked with had several characteristics in common. Among these was their ability to ADAPT to situations when necessary. Never refer to yourself or other salespeople as a lizard; however, there is one family of lizards that you should know about. They are CHAMELEONS. Cameleons are any of the numerous lizards characterized by their ability to change the color of their skin in order to adapt to the environment. Chameleons do not change what they are—they adapt.

Practitioners of NLP frequently refer to a principle from cybernetics called the "Law of Requisite Variety" which states:

> The part in a system, machine, or human inter-action that has the most flexibility will be the con-trolling part in that system.

In other words, if what you're doing isn't getting the response you want, it will help to have the flexibility to do something different!

Chameleons thrive because of their ability to "do something different"—to change their color to match their surroundings.

Successful salespeople thrive because they learn to adapt to the environment and react to prospects—they have the flexibility to change strategies when necessary.

Your prospects are at the middle of your implementation triangle, and reacting to your prospects is at the center of your peak performance in sales.

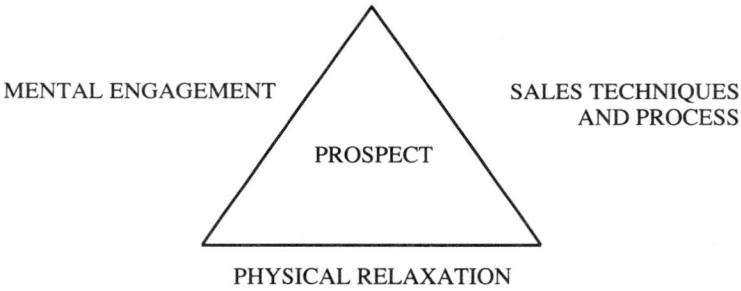

The Minnesota Fats Story

Minnesota Fats once remarked to me that one of the reason he was the world's best pool player was because he played the balls as he *found* them, not as he *wished* them to be. He reacted to the balls, the table, and the total environment in which he found them within his personal model of the real world. His game was not to act, but to react. As a result, Minnesota Fats played on the other side of ordinary performance and truly was one of the most remarkable pool players the game has ever known.

Part of the process of selling is learning to take situations as you *find* them, not as you *wish* them to be.

Your Prospects

Throughout the course of this book there will be several techniques you will want to develop into habits. One primary one should be observing and reacting to prospects. There are few better ways to learn about prospects than to observe and work with them. However, observing prospects does take time, structure, and practice in the laboratory of reality. Prospects are not good, not bad, just different, and THANKS FOR THE DIFFERENCES. In observing these differences, you are going to need some general direction.

First, add structure to your observations. While you cannot place prospects into exact categories, the variations become so extensive that you need a classification system.

Representational Systems

One of the best ways to observe people is to carefully watch their specific behavioral signals. Our senses—vision, touch, hearing, smell, and taste—are our "representational systems." They "represent" the world at large to our brain in the form of signals from our eyes, ears, etc. We then respond (behave) in reaction to these signals.

People take in, process, and respond to the data received via their representational systems in different ways—and these are the differences to watch for with your prospects.

"Barring neurological damage, we can see, feel, hear, smell, and taste. Each one of these sensory inputs has physical places in our brains to which the experience is sent, processed, and recorded. This assimilation of the initial input transforms the experience into something different from the original stimulus. What we actual-

ly perceive are representations or models of what
each of our sensory organs transmits to us. These
individual models of assimilation are called representational systems. At any moment we are receiving and processing input from all of our senses,
even when we are not consciously aware of it.
Each "slide out of time" is composed of the elements which make up the 4-tuple (4T) . . . Every
4T includes each of the representational systems:
sight is the "visual" system (V); feeling is the
"kinesthetic" system (K); hearing is the "auditory"
system (A); and smell and taste make up the "ol-
factory" system (O)."[1]

A vital part of developing skills of observation, or sensory acuity, will be to watch people's eyes. The eyes have
been called the "gateways to the soul," and reveal much
information about WHAT and HOW people are thinking.
There are other behavioral cues besides eye movements
that you can watch—breathing, body posture, and skin
color are just a few—but for now we will focus on "Eye
Accessing Cues."

"In the mid-1970's Bandler and Grinder (the
pioneers of NLP) began to study the patterns of
movements of people's eyes as people thought
and spoke. They discovered that these movements correlated fairly well with certain types of
information retrieval behaviors. These systematic
patterns of behavior were eventually formalized
into a model called accessing cues.
"When people are thinking and talking, they
move their eyes in what is known as eye-scanning
patterns. These movements appear to be
symptomatic of their attempts to gain access to internally stored or internally generated informa-

tion. This information is encoded in our minds in one or more of the representational systems. When a person "goes inside" to retrieve a memory or to create a new thought, he exhibits certain behaviors indicative of the representational systems he is accessing at the moment.

"When you observe people talking or thinking, you may notice their eyes constantly in motion, darting back and forth, up and down, occasionally glancing at objects and people but just as often "focused" on inner experiences. As previously mentioned, these movements are symptomatic of the way they are thinking. In the descriptions that follow, the word "looking" refers to the movement of a person's eyes in the direction indicated. "Left" means toward a person's left, and "right" means toward his right. It is helpful to keep in mind that this accessing behavior represents "looking" internally. That is, during the moment of information retrieval, people are generally not conscious of external visual stimuli. Rather, they are concentrating on internally stored or internally generated images, sounds, words, and feelings."

EYE ACCESSING CUES

Visual accessing cues for a "normally organized" right-handed person:

V^C Visual constructed images

V^R Visual remembered (eidetic) images

(Eyes defocused and unmoving also indicates visual accessing)

A^C Auditory constructed sounds or words

A^R Auditory remembered sounds or words

K Kinesthetic feelings (also smell and taste)

A Auditory sounds or words

LOOKING UP AND TO THE RIGHT— CONSTRUCTED IMAGES

These are visual images or pictures which are created by the individual. They can be recombinations of pieces of previously experienced visual input (see "eidetic images") into new or novel forms or sequences, or they can be created images which are constructed in response to other sensory stimuli. Constructed images are usually characterized by flatness or lack of depth and sometimes by a lack of color.

LOOKING UP AND TO THE LEFT— EIDETIC IMAGES

These are stored visual images or pictures of past events and other previously experienced visual stimuli. This includes dreams and constructed images that have already been experienced. These images are usually characterized by having both depth and motion— as in a movie—as well as color.

LOOKING LEVEL AND TO THE RIGHT— CONSTRUCTED SPEECH

This pattern is usually associated with the process of creating spoken language. In this position, the person is "putting into words" what he wants to say next.

LOOKING LEVEL AND TO THE LEFT— REMEMBERED SOUND

This includes such tonal representation as the "alphabet tune" and letters, advertisement jingles, phone numbers, and colloquialisms like slang and swearing. This is also where a person often moves his eyes when remembering auditory tape

loops; messages stored in short, often tuneful or
rhythmic patterns which have been so often
repeated that the person has lost conscious awareness of their existence. One example of this is the
"Remember-to-get-the-milk-on-the-way-home-
from-work" line that is recited so often during the
course of the morning that it eventually drops
from conscious awareness. (Note: the next two
eye-scanning patterns are often reversed in both
right- and left-handed people. It is important to
determine which pattern is being used by an individual before you can use the information
gained from observing these eye movements.)

LOOKING DOWN AND TO THE RIGHT— FEELINGS

In this position a person can access both
derived feelings (emotions) and stored kinesthetic memories. Think of the position you often
see a depressed person in: head bowed, shoulders
rounded, body drawn into itself. That person is
really "into his feelings." Remember that for
some individuals, accessing feelings will be down
and to the left.

LOOKING DOWN AND TO THE LEFT— INTERNAL DIALOG

Usually associated with "deep thought," these
are the words and sounds made internally that ac-
company this process. (At times, these sounds
and exclamations may "leak" out without a person being aware of it: "Please stop mumbling to
yourself" is an often heard response to this
leakage." Typically, internally dialog is a running
commentary on your current experience. At
quieter moments, it can be an analytic tool of

complex, rational, logical thinking. (This would be "rational" and "logical" only relative to the individual's model of reality, not necessarily to a general concensus of reality.) This accessing pattern may be down and to the right for some individuals.

DEFOCUSED EYES—VISUALIZATION
This may be in any of the above positions and is very often used during face-to-face conversations by individuals who communicate using the "look to listen" rule. This is usually accessing of either eidetic or constructed visual imagery. However, it may also indicate accessing of other forms of information.

CLOSED EYES—TASTE AND SMELL
Although people often close their eyes in order to remember a particular taste or smell, watch for movements of the eyes under the lids. These movements can indicate any of the previously discussed accessing cues and can be interpreted as if the eyes were open.[2]

Observing eye accessing cues is a useful method for gathering very specific information about someone at a given moment. It is one model that you can utilize. There are other models which provide more generalized systems of "personalities"—the complex sequences and patterns of behavior that people demonstrate on a continual basis.

Classification System: "DiSC" Needs Model

One classification system already in place is Performax Systems International, Inc.'s model, as found in its Personal

Profile System Instrument. In the remainder of this book this model will be refered to as the 'DiSC' system. While there are a variety of personality profiling systems on the market, we have examined most of them and found this one to be better suited to our specific sales training objectives.

The "DiSC" system contains four primary categories of needs-driven behavior. Value-driven behavior is a different discussion and is not included in this book.

Begin By Knowing Thyself

Socrates might well have initiated the trend of dealing with prospects by first understanding yourself when he penned those now famous words, "Know thyself."

"Know thyself" can even help you answer questions about prospect behavioral tendencies, sales styles, and other personality related issues. You can work along with us right now and learn a little about your own personality style in sales. The following is a sample of the 'DiSC' Personal Profile System and is not intended to take the place of the full profile or represent the Performax instrument. The intent of the following example is to give you some understanding of the profile itself, let you see how it applies to you personally, and to help you understand the prospect information presented in the remainder of this chapter.

In each of the five groupings below examine the four words and determine how closely each describes you in sales. Picture yourself in sales, not playing golf, or at home relaxing. In each grouping of words please rank all four words in the order they most nearly describe you. Rank them highest to lowest; 6 is the highest, 4 next, 2 follows, and O is lowest. Each group of words must be ranked 6, 4,

2, or O. No ties.

I can read your mind from here and the answer is yes! Not all of the words describe you and it is difficult to rank them in order. Go ahead and give it your best.

Example:

4	D. Self-reliant
2	I. Sociable
0	S. Patient
6	C. Soft-spoken

1. D. Self-reliant
   I. Sociable
   S. Patient
   C. Soft-spoken

2. D. Determined
   I. Convincing
   S. Good-natured
   C. Cautious

3. D. Competitive
   I. Charming
   S. Considerate
   C. Diplomatic

4. D. Pioneering
   I. Optimistic
   S. Accommodating
   C. Respectful

5. D. Risk-taker
   I. Fun loving
   S. Satisfied
   C. Accurate

Source: Adapted from Performax Systems International, Inc., Personal Profile System.

Now total all five of your responses to the "D" words and write that total in the space provided below. Now do the same for all the "I" words you marked, then the "S" words, and finally the "C" words. When you total your responses, they should total 6O. Please do your totaling now.

Your totals are: D___ I___ S___ C___ =_____ (6O)

What Do These Totals Mean?

They mean that each salesperson can be different in their approach to sales based on their individual personalities. This short quiz is not the important part; the discussion and learning that can follow is.

Research supports the conclusion that the most effective salespeople are those who "know themselves," understand the demands of the situations at hand, and can adapt to meet them. They know their own decision-making strategies and preferred representational systems. When you participate in the real challenge of sales you are adapting to change constantly. Understanding yourself can be the first step in the process of adapting to change and to a variety of sales situations.

The following descriptions were written with your prospects in mind, but you can discover information about yourself as well. When you have a "D" score higher than 15, you typically will have more of the "D" tendencies described below. The same is true for the "I", "S", and "C" tendencies. When your score is less than 15, you typically have less of the tendency described.

"Dominance" Type Behaviors

This category includes the tendencies of such individuals to change things within their environment to overcome difficulties. Keep in mind that prospects will not be walking around with a big "Dominance" or "D" stapled in the middle of their backs. We are only talking about prospect's observable behavioral tendencies.

Some of the "Dominance" or "D" tendencies include:

IN SALES	IN SPORTS
-- Not only enjoys winning, but beating the competition is important -- Typically in a big hurry	-- It's not how you play the game that counts. Winning is what really counts! -- They run most of the time

"Influencing" Type Behaviors

Here the emphasis is on changing things within the environment to gain compliance or agreement. Individuals with influencing tendencies sure seem to have a good time accomplishing this objective. Some of the "Influencing" or "I" tendencies include:

IN SALES	IN SPORTS
-- May talk their way out of more sales than into them -- Enjoy meeting new people -- Go with their feelings -- Enjoy winning	-- They not only play, they lead the cheering -- We won, so let's have a party. Oh, we lost! Well, let's have a party anyway.

"Steadiness" Type Behaviors

Individuals with this major drive are typically motivated by the goal of steadiness. They like to continue in established patterns. They strive to cooperate with the forces in their environment. Some of the "Steadiness" or "S" tendencies include:

IN SALES

-- Likes to stay with old and familiar customers
-- Very systematic in and with the sales process
-- Likes to continue using familiar sales techniques and practices

IN SPORTS

-- A team player
-- May not play if it takes too much time away from their key groups (family, friends, etc.)

"Compliance" Type Behaviors

Individuals with this major drive are typically motivated by the goal of compliance. Compliance is typically with their own standards. High compliance individuals typically focus on working towards perfection while keeping the forces within their environment under control. (Perfectionism and control are some of the characteristics of "left brain" functions—behaviors controlled to a great degree by the left hemisphere of the brain.) Some of the "Compliance" or "C" tendencies include:

IN SALES	IN SPORTS
-- Follows key rules and processes -- Very cautious in approaching prospects -- Desire facts and bases personal decisions on logic	-- Keep score and diplomatically reminds others of the rules if necessary -- If they are going to play, their perspective is to do it right or not to play at all

There you have it, the start of your prospect classification system. You will be working on, and with, this system for all of your sales career. This is your beginning.

What You Already Know

In our sales seminars we pause at this point and let participants see just how much they *already* know about how a prospect classification system such as "DiSC" works and how their prospects fit into their new classification system.

As we work through the "DiSC" classification system keep your own prospects in mind. For the purposes of this discussion, individual sales calls are not good or bad. Instead, some are just more appropriate with certain groups. It is important to be aware of the distinctions all prospects make in their own personal definition between a "good" salesperson and a "good" sales call. As we work through the four prospect groups in your classification system we will be looking at both prospect buying habits and how they view you, the salesperson.

In the following example, we use the field of real estate. You can mentally insert your own prospects and products as you go through the exercises.

High "Dominance"/"D" Tendencies

This group is dominant and tends to act quickly. During one of our seminars someone asked if a prospect had ever purchased a home the first time they saw it. One real estate salesperson related an instance where a man actually purchased a home without even seeing it. In retrospect the salesperson calculated that the man had to have had very high dominance tendencies.

Prospects high in this tendency may tell you they want to see twenty houses the first day, tell you they will know the house they want when they see it, and expect you to buy lunch. To them, a good sales call is when they are in control. Leave the driving to their "ego" and you will have a better opportunity for a decision in your favor later.

In the space below, write in the major behavior tendencies you see in your high "D" prospects.

_____

_____

_____

_____

High "Influencing"/"I" Tendencies

Prospects high in this tendency can be real dreamers, especially when it comes to purchasing their "dream" home. They spend a lot of time visiting and using different representational systems, perhaps even auditorily day-dreaming (visualizing in their inner mind, with intense kinesthetic feelings) with you about the type of home they want. You will notice that they are typically optimistic, verbal, trusting, and non-detail oriented. (Being non-detail oriented is one of the characteristics of "right brain" functions—behaviors controlled to a great degree by the right hemisphere of the brain.) Allow these prospects time to dream, but keep both of your own feet planted firmly on the ground, as you will need to provide some order to their decision-making process.

This group enjoys "smelling the roses" as they look at homes.

In the space below, write in the major behavior tendencies you see in your high "I" prospects.

_____

_____

_____

_____

High "Steadiness"/"S" Tendencies

With these prospects, known facts and figures are likely to become a key factor for the first time. They may very well show up at your office with a notebook full of information and a shopping plan already drawn out. Remember, they like order and structure in their lives. They may even have their own checklist, with ten copies for the day, of things to look for in their new home. Their decision-making process is likely to be slow, thorough, and organized. They will probably tend to be "visual" people (they will have a preference for the visual representational system), will look at things carefully, and will want neatness and organization. They are typically warm people, so slow down and allow yourself to enjoy them and the selling process.

In the space below, write in the major behavior tendencies you see in your high "S" prospects:

_____

_____

_____

_____

High "Compliance"/"C" Tendencies

You will find that prospects high in this tendency do not like to make mistakes. They will often postpone a decision until all of the facts are in—and that means all the facts and related considerations. They are the people who show up at a new house with a flashlight, crawl around in every corner, and find things that even the inspector missed. They can be thorough! They are very diplomatic, but be certain to answer all of their questions, or get the answers for them. When you do not know something do not fake it; high "C's" will find out what they need to know one way or another.

In the space below, write in the behavior tendencies of your high "C" prospects.

_____

_____

_____

_____

You cannot know too much about your prospects. Prospect knowledge is one area that successful salespeople work on for all of their career.

Preparation And Habit

Two key words in peak performance for any walk of life are:

PREPARATION

HABIT

The "prospect classification" skills just presented will not just come to you one day while you are out on a sales calls. Before the sale call is when you develop the habits and knowledge bases you will need for effective selling. Effective selling is reacting, not acting.

Learning to identify and minimize potential conflicts with prospects is a major part of "Chameleon" skills. Listed below are people and work behavioral characteristics relating to compatibility that you can study and implement as part of your inter-personal sales skill set.

COMPATIBILITY CHARACTERISTICS

DISC Styles	Excellent		Good		Fair		Poor	
	1	2	3	4	5	6	7	8
D & D				x	*			
D & I			x		*			
D & S	*					x		
D & C						*		x
I & I	x					*		
I & S	*				x			
I & C			*					x
S & S	x	*						
S & C	x	*						
C & C	x	*						

X - Human Relations
* - Work Tasks

In implementing the information on this chart, it does not mean that with high compliance behavioral tendencies you are always going to experience difficulty selling to an individual with high dominance tendencies. It does *indicate* that a more effective posture for working with this individual can come from influencing behavioral tendencies.

The steps involved in implementing the information just presented include:

- 1. Knowing your own behavioral tendencies.
- 2. Developing the skill to observe and draw conclusions from the behaviors and communication strategies of others.
- 3. Being aware of "potential" conflicts with others.
- 4. Developing the behavioral flexibility necessary to work effectively in a given environment.

The action you decide to take in #4 is all up to you. Ask yourself one key question: are my chances of getting prospects to make a decision in my favor better in a mode of conflict and disagreement or harmony and rapport? The answer to that question is up to you.

When a great golfer like Doug Sanders changes his golf swing to hit a low shot into the wind, or Pete Rose takes a little off his swing to hit a low outside curve ball, they are ADAPTING to their environment, not attempting to change it to meet their desires.

Often you experience prospects who are different from yourself, or different from others with whom you are comfortable. You feel uncomfortable changing for them. You can begin to think, "What, me change? Why don't they change once in a while!" That level of thinking can progress very quickly to, "I'm just who I am and if they don't like it, then it's tough!" From this level of thinking losing the sale is just one step away.

The words you think about are very important here.

For instance, take the word "change" and replace it with "adapt." How does that feel to you? Go ahead, try it on for size. We are not asking you to change. We are suggesting that you adapt to the prospect and the environment. If you attempted to change your basic individuality with each client, not only would you experience undue personal distress, but you would compromise one of your strongest assets—the real you! We want you to maintain your "core," your real self.

Performax said it very well when they wrote:

"All of us have developed behavioral patterns—distinct ways of thinking, feeling, and acting. The central core of our patterns tends to remain stable because it reflects our individual identities. However, the demands of the work environment often require different responses that evolve into a work behavioral style."

Your objective will be to work towards a greater understanding of yourself and prospects in a sales environment. Focus initially on yourself and determine the sales environment that is most conducive to your personal success and peak performance. When you find yourself ineffective in sales, it might be that you are in an inappropriate type of sales position. Remember, just as you have an individual profile, sales jobs have individual profiles also.

We know that the most effective salespeople are those who learn about themselves, sell within an environment where they can function effectively, learn the demands of prospects, and then adapt their sales strategies and techniques to meet those demands.

Your objectives for this section can be summarized as follows:

- 1. First identify your own dominant sales style behaviors.
- 2. Find the sales environment most appropriate to your individual style and peak performance.
- 3. Expand your understanding and appreciation for different behavioral styles and ways of processing information among prospects.
- 4. Develop your flexibility to adapt to a variety of prospects by multiple sales styles.

**FLEXIBILITY IS IN THE MIND
AS WELL AS IN THE BODY.**

For additional information on the *Performax Personal Profile System (DiSC)*, and related materials, you can contact Jim Robertson through Metamorphous Press, P.O. Box 10616, Portland, Oregon, 97210-0616 or call 1-800-937-7771.

References

[1]Byron Lewis & Frank Pucelik, *Magic Demystified* (Portland, OR: Metamorphous Press, 1982) p. 31-32.
[2]Byron Lewis & Frank Pucelik, *Magic Demystified* (Portland, OR: Metamorphous Press, 1982) p. 116-120.

5

There is Your Side and Then There Is The Right Side

The Sales Process

Early in a sales career, it is not uncommon for sales-people to get into disagreements (well, discussions) with prospects. Fortunately it does not take most people new to sales long to realize that there are always two side to every discussion. There is the salesperson's side and then there is the "right" side, the prospect's side—at least it is "right" in the prospect's model of reality.

From your "DiSC Prospect Classification" System you recall that prospects have their own models of reality and that we all "create our own reality." This being the case, let's look at the sales process from your side, and then from the right side, the prospect's side.

The terms used to describe the sales process from your side are typically:

Approach

|

Fact Finding

|

Presentation

Handling Objections

|

Closing the Sale

|

Follow up

Every sales trainer learns to present these five elements just a little differently. Some of us even add additional steps such as Pre-Approach, Follow up, etc. If we didn't make these distinctions, companies wouldn't need as many different sales trainers and more of us would be out of work. Therefore, the variations of these terms among various sales trainers and sales training programs are limitless, but that is not the issue.

May I ask you a question? What seems inappropriate to you about these steps? Read back through the terms once more before answering.

By now you have the answer. The terms used to describe the previous steps place the emphasis back on you, the salesperson, and not where it belongs, on the prospect.

YOU approach the prospect
YOU initiate fact-finding
YOU make a presentation
YOU handle objections
YOU close the sale.

These words may not be wrong, they just create an inappropriate FOCUS for the sales process. There is that word again, focus.

To sell more effectively let's put the focus back on the prospect and view the process from their side. The words labeling the steps in the buying cycle from the prospect's perspective can include:

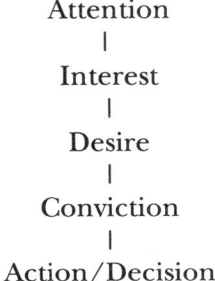

Attention
|
Interest
|
Desire
|
Conviction
|
Action/Decision

This is the prospect's decision-making strategy en route to advancing from prospect to customer. It makes little difference whether you are selling a 747 or a package of chewing gum, the PROCESS of decision-making for prospects is fundamentally the same. Granted, prospects take different amounts of time within certain steps, move from step-to-step at their own pace, and go back through certain steps. Prospects will also make decisions using various strategies that correlate with their preferred representational system. For now, however, we want you to focus on the process from the prospect's perspective, not the relative importance of each step.

Consumer Decision Process

As you look for a more complete explanation of consumer behavior, the writings of Dr. Roger Blackwell can be very helpful.

An oversimplication of Dr. Blackwell's consumer decision making model is as follows:

Arousal & Perception
|
Comparison
|
Problem Recognition

Search For Alternatives
|
Evaluation of Alternatives
|
Decision Process
|
Outcomes

(Postpurchase Evaluation & Further Behavior) Source: Blackwell, Roger D., James F. Engel, David T. Kollat, Consumer Behavior, Holt, Rinehart and Winston, Inc., 1968.

Form New Habits

Begin right now to change the words you use and form new habits in mentally "imaging" and verbally describing the sales process. The words you use are key. Words prompt images (as well as associated sounds and feelings), and by now you know that images are you.

Take just a second to consider some of the images your old sales terms can prompt.

Would you like to have your objections "handled" by a perfect stranger? Prospects do not want strangers handling anything of theirs.

During the fact-finding stage of a sale, would you like to have "probing" techniques used on you? Doctors probe, dentists probe, and missiles probe the new frontiers of space, but I am not certain that prospects want to be probed by salespeople.

Here is another great one. We work and work in preparation for the sales call, make the initial appointment, go to considerable lengths in making the sales call, and then our primary objective is to "close" the sale. Remember, words prompt images. We close doors, we close the casket at a funeral, and a missile might close in on its target, but in sales isn't our primary objective to "open" a business and professional relationship? The words we use are important. Here is our vocabulary switch:

OLD WORDS	NEW WORDS
Approach	Attention
Fact-Finding	Interest
Presentation	Desire
	Conviction
Handling Objections	Questions
Closing The Sale	Decision/Action

After reading books on consumer behavior and decision making by individuals including Dr. Blackwell, you may wish to refine your list of NEW WORDS that describe the buying process. Keep them in a place where you will see them daily and begin to integrate them.

A Living System

Effective sales calls are alive! Creative sales calls live, flow, develop, and are always changing. They are not a preprogrammed set of steps within an isolated environment that the salesperson or prospect must go through. On certain sales calls you will be confronted with a major question or objection the very minute you walk through a prospect's door. On other sales calls you will never get a question.

During one of our training programs, a real estate agent told us of receiving a phone call from a prospect. The prospect knew exactly the house he wanted and the decision was made right then and there to purchase. Sarah commented that she almost lost the sale because she kept wanting to do more for the prospect, get him to fly in to look at more houses, or just look over the area first. Prospects do not just call up and purchase a home!

Sarah's case was the rare exception, but the example of her high "D" prospect does illustrate the point that sales calls do not fit into nice formal patterns. They are dynamic and require a high degree of behavioral flexibility.

Jerry was in that same workshop and provided an example at the opposite end of the spectrum. He had been working with a prospect for close to three months when he finally helped the prospect to the point where the prospect was ready to take action. Then the high "C" of the prospect and his lawyer took over and believe it or not it took an additional six months to get the contracts worked out. This is another rare exception, but truth can be stranger than fiction.

Although each sales call is dynamic and unique, all elements of the prospect's buying process will be a part of each sale. From your side of the buying process, the elements or steps in the process provide you with a roadmap for effective selling. By first understanding and being able to use each techniques within each element effectively, you can then advance to personalizing your sales calls and developing an effective style with a wider range of prospects.

Keep Words In Their Proper Perspective

This book was designed to lead you at least a little ways away from what is typically seen as the NORMAL approach to sales and as such certain additional issues of importance to peak performance must be presented. In the beginning of this chapter we ask you to begin making a major shift in the words you use to describe the steps in the process of a sale. It is vital that you realize the significance in the words

you use to describe a sale, the sales process, and the work
you are about to undertake.

Words Are "Maps"

Words are only symbols for experience, they are not
experience. In fact, by analyzing the structure of language,
and why humans use it, we find that words are several levels
removed from the "real" world!

Linguists and psychologists have studied the structure
of language and identified distinct levels within our experience of living. Each level is a representation or model
of the next.

Language
Experience of experience
Sensory experience
World at Large[1]

An example might be a child who curiously puts his
hand on a hot burner. First, he has a sensory experience:
he feels the burner and the heat. Then, his "experience of
experience" is the process of translating the feelings in his
fingers into pain and alarm. Finally, his feelings are repre-
sented with language and he screams, "OUCH!"

Words are complex tools to describe our experiences,
but they are not the experience itself. A good analogy is a
map. A streetmap, for example, is not actually a city, but
rather a model or representation of a city, and is useful in
getting you where you want to go.

Understanding the relationship between words and
"reality" is crucial in your growth toward peak performance
in your career. The words we use are the maps of our lives,
and if we are to arrive at the place we want to go, we need

to use accurate maps.

Referring back to your 'DiSC' prospect identification technique, you learned that the words "effective salesperson" have a totally different meaning to each classification of prospect. The same words evoke an almost entirely different experience base from each person or group.

How might individuals with different profile tendencies describe a "good" salesperson? Prospects with high dominance ("D") tendencies may hold an image of good as providing fast service and quick results. Prospects with high influencing ("I") tendencies may formulate a friendly and more verbal image for a good salesperson. Systematic ("S") prospects may hold a view of working with the salesperson as a team member, while those with conforming ("C") tendencies hold yet another view that includes a good salesperson as one who follows a standard operating procedure. All of these are different images evoked by the same word, "good." Yet each view is equally as realistic to the group or individual holding that perspective.

As important as words are, psycholinguists report that in the act of one person attempting to communicate an IDEA to another, the spoken word carries as little as 7% of the total meaning. That is not much! Therefore, we want you processing images. Images are how you think. Images are you. Just as important, images are how your prospects think, process information, and make decisions.

Think about images for just a minute. Selling is not an activity that you are simply out there doing to or with someone else. Selling is a process and you are part of the total. Just as you do not merely live in the environment, you are part of that environment. You do not make a sale; you are the sale. Think about being part of the sale until you can see yourself there, inside the process in the here-and-now, not just standing outside of the process and "making" a sale.

Image Your Way Through A Sale

In place of discussing what we think are the appropriate steps in a sale, image your way through a sale and see what you come up with. The NLP reference for this process is called "Future Pacing." This is when you have identified a behavior that you want to habituate. You generate an image or movie of yourself in a future situation where that behavior will be appropriate; then you visualize yourself successfully performing the behavior. This is "practicing for the future." You can devote more time to developing each phase of the sale later, but for right now, prepare to take a mini-trip through a sale with imagery. As with your relaxation techniques and exercises, you may want someone to take you through this one the first time, or you can pre-record it.

- Get in a quiet place, relax, and begin breathing deeply.
- You are calm, quiet, relaxed and ready to begin your sales call.
- You are mentally in front of a familiar client's building. You see yourself enter the building. Watch as you go in.
- You are walking to his office.
- See him in his office. Is he standing or sitting?
- He sees you and invites you in. Listen to him invite you in. What does his voice sound like? Is he smiling?
- This is a client you have worked with before. Take a moment and notice the surroundings, all of them. There is a certain feeling in the air. Feel it. There is even a dominant smell. What does it smell like? Coffee? Cologne? Dust?
- There is one particular color that stands out for you. See that color.

- You hear many sounds. Pick out one and listen to it for a minute. Do you hear traffic? Mozart? A jackhammer?
- Observe what the individual is wearing. Allow all of your senses to function. Process the sounds, sights, tastes, smells, and even the touch of the surroundings. Are you sitting in a leather sofa? Touching an oak desk?
- You are calm, quiet, and relaxed.
- Image yourself approaching the individual. Notice your body position. Notice his. You are not in the environment; you are the environment. You are relaxed.
- Hear and feel the easy flow of conversation from two people who already know each other. You have your prospect's attention and the communication is easy.
- Notice the expression of interest on his face. See interest being expressed through his new body position. You can hear interest in the tone and pitch of his voice. He is leaning forward, gesturing, and his face has a warm color to it. He is interested because he is talking about something that is interesting to him.
- You are calm, quiet, and relaxed.
- He is doing the talking. You are listening. Observe as he continues talking.
- The value of your product becomes clear to your prospect.
- Observe his expression change. His eyes look up. He is thinking. You are calm and he is giving you additional feedback. Through your senses, you know he is convincing himself that your product can satisfy his needs. You are quiet and sitting back and observing the entire process. You are breathing deeply and you are relaxed. Observe as he becomes

more and more convinced.

- Remain relaxed and process the remainder of your conversation with him.
- You sense an expression of joy. He has shown you that he not only needs what you have to offer, but he wants it as well.
- You are the environment. Remain in touch with it and continue processing through all of your senses. Notice his feelings of satisfaction with having found a solution to a problem.
- Finally you see an action that lets both you and the prospect know that a mutually acceptable decision has been made. You know he is making a commitment to you and to your product. Observe how you know this. Quietly observe the action. You are calm, quiet, and relaxed.
- You are breathing deeply. You are very conscious of your breathing.
- Your prospect has become a customer.
- You open your eyes and are aware of all that just transpired in your sales call.

Now that you have completed the exercise please continue on and record the experience in the space provided.

Plan on going through this exercise at least once a month for the remainder of your sales career. It is effective imagery practice, a productive review of your sales strategies, and a valid learning and review process.

Your Experience

Now is the time to record your experience from the sales call. You were on the sales call. Record the experience below.

Describe the following about the sales call you just made:

The environment I found myself in was:

_____

_____

_____

_____

_____

The sense of relaxation I felt was:

_____

_____

_____

_____

_____

I would describe the customer/prospect I saw as:

_____

_____

_____

_____

_____

I knew he was interested in my offer because:

_____

_____

_____

_____

_____

I knew when he had made his decision because:

_____

_____

_____

_____

Blocking Out Does Not Work

Don't think of the color red!
Don't see a red car!
What happened? Exactly! You saw a red car.
Don't hit the golf ball in the water! Whatever you do, don't hit the ball in the water to the right. You will lose the match for sure if you hit the ball to the right!
Where did you just set yourself up to hit the golf ball? Exactly! You lost another golf ball because you just hit the golf ball to the right and into the water.

DON'T BLOW THE SALE
This sale is a must to make quota!
Just don't blow this one!
Just don't get too excited!
Don't let the prospect know that you need this one!
Your job depends on it!
Your career depends on it!
Your life depends on it!

What happened? Correct again. You just gave yourself very specific instructions on how to lose the sale.

It Also Happens In The World Of Sports

It's the bottom of the ninth inning, the World Series of baseball, New York against Milwaukee. Milwaukee is batting and has two outs and two strikes on the batter. The coach calls time, walks out to the pitcher's mound and tells the pitcher, "Whatever you do, don't pitch him high and outside."
"Don't pitch him high and outside." "High and outside." "High and outside." The pitcher moves into the stretch and takes his windup. His brain is working and his

body is paying full attention. The pitcher's brain continues to process the words "high and outside," and you know the rest of the story. The pitch is delivered high and outside, the batter connects for an extra run, New York loses.

The mind does not think in the reverse of what you give it to process. It cannot process a "negative command." It processes information literally. "Don't think of a red pumpkin on a skateboard" becomes translated by your brain into the command THINK OF A RED PUMPKIN ON A SKATEBOARD. "Don't do" and "do" are exactly the same to your mind. The brain strips off the "don't" and away it goes, doing everything in its power to complete the image you have painted.

The solution is to REPLACE negative images with positive images.

Don't Think Pink Elephants!

There, you did it again. You just saw a pink elephant. So, what is the solution?

YOU DO NOT STOP UNPRODUCTIVE HABITS, YOU BUILD NEW ONES.

This is a very important statement for sales and for all of life. You say to yourself, "stop eating" and what are you imaging? That's right, you see yourself eating again. But you go on and give even more detailed instructions to yourself. "Stop eating that favorite double chocolate chocolate chip ice cream that is rich, smooth, creamy, melts in your mouth, and makes you feel good over. The one you can see yourself holding in your hand right now. That's right, stop eating the one thing that makes eating worth while!" And on and on you go.

To be more effective in controlling your weight, your images of being thin and feeling better have to be stronger than your images of consuming large amounts of specific food items.

"Stop smoking." This is another great mistake. You say "stop smoking" to yourself and what are your images? That's right, you think of smoking.

YOU DO NOT STOP UNPRODUCTIVE IMAGES, YOU BUILD NEW ONES. Use this space to keep a running replacement of negative words.

Negative Words	Positive Replacements
Bad	Inappropriate
"Close the sale"	Decision in our favor
Pitch	_____
Handle objections	Answer questions
Deal	_____
"Stupid" prospect	_____
"NO"	_____
Failure	_____

(add some of your own)

_____	_____
_____	_____
_____	_____

Vague Words	More Specific
Hope	It will happen
Try	_____
Sale	_____
If	_____

(add some of your own)

_____	_____
_____	_____
_____	_____

Focus on new and more positive replacement words and phrases.

Instead of trying to stop old and unproductive habits that keep you from selling effectively, focus your attention on building stronger and more productive habits.

Dead Man Test

Some salespeople, and sales managers, would benefit from applying the Dead Man Test to their efforts at talking to themselves and others. The Dead Man Test works this way: when a dead person can meet the directions you are giving him, then the instructions are incomplete in that they do not adequately specify HOW TO DO SOMETHING CORRECTLY and they cause you to focus on the negative aspects of the task at hand.

Consider how often you give this type of direction to yourself and others.

"Stop getting excited!" Well, a dead person could do that.

"Stop thinking that way. That is just like you!"

"Quit being so negative!"

A dead person could follow any of these instructions because they specify only the elimination of certain behaviors or thoughts without specifying positive behavioral choices.

The key is in developing positive expectations. One method for developing and accomplishing positive expectations is through effective goal setting and planned activities.

A Mini-Lesson On Goal Setting

While the objective of the chapter is not to teach you goal setting, a review of the following principles can support your efforts.

- Set individual goals over group or company goals.
- Set challenging goals over easy goals.
- Set realistic over unrealistic goals.
- Set specific goals over general goals.
- Set immediate, short-term, and long-term goals.
- Set your goals down in writing.
- And perhaps most important, set performance goals over outcome goals.

And remember those wise words from *The One Minute Golfer:*

All Good Performances
Start With Clear Goals
and
Start Right Now

References

[1] Kim Kostere and Linda Malatesta, *Maps, Models and the Structure of Reality* (Portland, OR: Metamorphous Press, 1991).

6

In This I Believe

Your Intent For Sales and the
Attention Step of The Sale

SALES CYCLE   PROSPECT
                                     BUYING CYCLE

┌──────→ Approach • • • • • • • • • • Attention ←──┐
├──────→ Fact Finding • • • • • • • • • Interest ←──┤
├→ Presentation/Recommendation • • • • Conviction ←─┤
├──────→ Handling Objections • • • • • • • Desire ←──┤
└──────→ Closing the Sale • • • • • • • • Action ←──┘

During his tenure as Chairman of the Board of Ford Motor Company, Phillip Caldwell made a presentation entitled, "In This I Believe." What impressed me most about Mr. Caldwell's presentation was the strength with which he held and expressed his convictions. Not everyone at Ford may have agreed with Mr. Caldwell, but they certainly knew what he stood for. He had taken a stand that centered around a very firm belief system. Phillip Caldwell stood for something and he let people know it.

In talking with one of my prior college business students, Akitoshi Horiuchi, about Mr. Caldwell's presentation, Aki commented how common such a statement was in Japan. "Before you go to work for a Japanese company" said Aki, "one of the first things you read is the statement of philosophy written by the head of that company. You do NOT seek a career with a firm without knowing, and being in agreement with, their major purpose for being in business." Aki told me that the heads of most major firms in Japan write entire books on the philosophies they hold for their organizations and their people.

Attention Step

The purpose of this step in the sales process is to begin building rapport between you and your prospect. Here is where the prospect must begin liking you, trusting you at a conscious and unconscious level, and getting himself ready to listen to you later in the sale. This is when you use "rapport building skills" that come from your careful observations and sensory cues. What words and key phrases does the prospect use? What does his nonverbal language tell you? How does he "image"? This is the "sale before the sale," and your first impression.

Your Name On The Marquee

Take this time to create a new image for yourself. You just found out that next Saturday night you are being honored at a banquet for your accomplishments in sales. Outside the banquet hall, on the marquee for all the world to see, will be written your statement of PURPOSE for your years in sales. What will you have them write?

Do not wait for your retirement banquet to write your statement of purpose. This is one of the most important statements you will ever write. Before the sun sets tonight begin writing down your statement of belief. Say it to yourself. Get an internal representation of it, check how your belief feels and how it sounds to yourself and others. You may not finish it tonight, but begin writing your own version of "In This I Believe."

This will be a statement of your intent, your purpose, your reason for selling. When your purpose is not straight with the world, you will not be straight with the world. Your intentions and belief systems will not be congruent with your behavior. MORE SALES PEOPLE ENTER AND LEAVE THE FIELD OF SALES FOR LACK OF HAVING SEARCHED OUT AND LIVED BY A VALID STATEMENT OF PURPOSE THAN FOR ANY OTHER REASON.

Your statement of purpose is not how you function; it goes far beyond that. This is your function, your identity, and your reason for choosing a pathway to professional fulfillment through sales.

Marquee Exercise

You may want to have someone read the following section to you, or you might want to pre-record it. Be certain to read it calmly and slowly.

- You provide your own purpose for sales. You write your own statement. You formulate the images that depict your purpose. Images come to you from within. Enter an "associated state" of mind and "go inside" your thoughts.
- Go to a quiet place. Your place. See, hear and feel your surroundings.

- Relax. Close your eyes.
- Become fully conscious of your breathing. Breathe in for six heart beats, breathe out for six, in for six, and continue breathing.
- You are calm, quiet, and relaxed. You are only conscious of your breathing.
- Now begin to change the image you see in your mind, as if you were turning the dials of a picture on a screen.
- Move slowly out and away from your body. See yourself from a distance. View the scene very clearly, yet remain at a distance. Disassociate from the image of yourself.
- Quietly notice one of your most valued customers. Observe the environment. Relax. Walk around. Observe the scene from all sides. Move the total scene until it is ten feet from you. You are calm, quiet, and relaxed. The scene stops. All images are stopped. Now an inner part, the part of you that helps you identify purposes and goals, finds a voice to speak with and asks you,"Why are you with that customer?"
- The voice asks yet another question, "What gives you the right to be with that customer?"
- You are calm, quiet, and relaxed.
- Allow an image or your answer to form. The question echoes through the walls of your mind. "Why am I here?" "What gives me the right to be with this customer?"
- You are calm, quiet, and relaxed. Allow the image to form.
- "What is my purpose? What purpose explains my being in sales?" Process the full effect of the images associated with your response to this question. Do not "look" for an answer, just be aware of the images that come to you. Let them happen. Pay attention

to the feelings. Acknowledge the forms. Process the images. Allow the images to flow.
- You are calm, quiet, and relaxed.

Allow yourself time with this exercise. Once the images begin to flow, allow them to go where they will. Do not act. Allow things to happen and your thoughts to flow. The first time through this exercise you may invest three minutes, perhaps five the next, then ten. Allow images and impressions to happen.

Your Images

Once you are through relaxing and have completed your images, describe them in writing. This can be the beginning of your personal statement. At first your images may be incomplete, but with practice they will fill out.

This is another exercise to do every month or so. Put this exercise on a planned schedule that fits your needs.

I was with that prospect because:

_____

_____

_____

_____

_____

I have the right to call on any prospect because:

_____

_____

_____

_____

_____

My purpose for being in sales is:

_____

_____

_____

_____

_____

When they write that one sentence on the marquee about my career in sales, it will say:

_____

_____

_____

_____

_____

This drill/exercise is an excellent candidate for an on-going mental exercise for getting to, and remaining at, a peak level of performance in sales. It is paramount that you do not accept other's opinions as to why you should, or should not, be in sales. This is a discovery journey you must travel alone. Listen from within and react.

"Should do" is another of those killer phrases to be avoided. "Should" and "ought" fall into the NLP definition of "Modal Operators of Necessity." This means that the statement you just made is an absolute "must" to you. The way to elicit choices for behavior is to switch the sentence around and ask yourself, "What would happen if I didn't. . .?" For example, if you habitually tell yourself, "I should call my mother every week," you can break the "absoluteness" of this sentence and give yourself more alternatives by asking, "What would happen if I didn't call my mother every week?" Then you can work with real behavior, not imagined "shoulds" and the feelings they may be associated with.

The Attention Step Of The Sale

Now you will shift your thinking from your INtention for being in sales to the ATtention Step in the sales process.

1. INtention is a matter of your direction and priority for being in the profession of sales and for a specific sales call.
2. ATtention is a matter of focus and what items receive and hold your interest.

Keep in mind that you have your set of intentions and attention, and the prospects have theirs.

This is an important enough concept for sales that it requires at least one example to ensure that we are both using the same definitions when we talk about intention and attention. For years we have been telling people in the world of sales, as well as the world of sports, to "concentrate." In a recent seminar we asked twenty participants to define that term and not only was each definition different from the other, but all of the definitions centered around the concept of "blocking out." Remember "don't think of pink elephants"? That is blocking out. We now know one thing—blocking out is not effective.

In that same sports psychology training clinic a very successful high school golf coach provided us with a clear and concise example of intention and attention.

Example: When playing a shot into a green the coach describes his golfer's INTENT to be getting the golf ball into the hole. He then instructs them on the use and development of concrete imagery skills to see the ball going into the hole, the roll of the ball on the green, the ball flight that it took to produce that roll, the club swing that it took to produce that ball flight, and then the player simply steps into the center of the swing and repeats it. Their intent is defined by the outcome and their reactions in producing that outcome.

The ATTENTION part of the formula that the coach teaches is for his players to remain in the here-and-now, associated, and remain focused on the task at hand. When the player brings back memories of the missed shot on the last hole, the ball they lost on number two, or the speeding ticket they got on the way to the golf match they are not in the here-and-now. When that same player constructs mental images of the future, to winning or losing the match, getting their picture in the newspaper, or going before the judge to pay that speeding ticket they are not in the here-and-now. Their primary task is to remain focused on the here-and-now and on the task at hand.

Your intent during the sales process can be:

_____

_____

_____

_____

_____

Your attention during the sales process can be:

_____

_____

_____

_____

_____

Attention is also a sense of focus and readiness on the part of your prospect. When you were driving your car in the earlier mental exercise and hit the telephone pole, your focus was on the rain, not the road. When you enter a prospect's office, their focus is on their road and their priorities, not yours. In gaining a prospect's attention you are actually helping them to change their focus. You are getting them prepared or receptive to listening to you later in the sales process.

Always ask yourself this question, "When I walk into that prospect's office, where is their attention focused?" In this first step in the buying cycle, not only are you preparing the prospect to listen to you later in the buying process, but this is your sale before the sale. It is right now that you begin earning the right to advance beyond this step. You only have one chance to make a first impression, and right here is where you begin selling yourself. Your INtent is going to come through to the prospect loud and clear from the very second that you step through their door. You are always communicating. Think about this statement for just a minute: "While with a prospect you are always communicating and cannot not communicate."

The Attention Step has two primary objectives. They are to:

1. Clear your prospects' minds of other issues and get them ready to listen you, which is a matter of focus, and

2. Allow you to begin selling yourself.

One effective strategy for gaining their attention is to talk with prospects about something in which they are interested. This is as old as the hills but still effective. This is part of gaining rapport with the prospect, getting them to a comfortable place where they feel, "This person is like me." What you are actually doing is giving the prospect time to change gears from what they were focused on when you entered their environment.

Information you have gained in the Preparation Step will help determine what topic you bring up during this step of the process. It may be their hobby, their family, a recent accomplishment, their business, their industry, but the emphasis is on "their," not "your". One way to pick topics is to listen to the words the prospect uses the most. Is he sound oriented? Does he use phrases like, "I hear you saying that you . . ." or "That rings a bell"? If so, his preferred representational system is auditory. You will probably gain a lot of rapport with this prospect by talking about music, concerts, or a speaker that he recently heard.

Guidelines For The Attention Step

1. Do not stay in this step too long. You are there as a professional salesperson, not as a professional visitor. Become a problem solver, not an interruption.

2. Learn the effect your clothing and appearance have on others and dress accordingly. Is your appearance congruent with your manner? How does your appearance affect your rapport with your prospect?

3. Learn the effect your body language has on others and again, act accordingly. Practitioners of NLP have entire libraries of information on nonverbal language, but for now, remember that "mirroring" or "matching" the nonverbal behavior of others helps to build rapport with them, if it is done respectfully and subtlely.

4. Keep your enthusiam one level, but no more, above the prospect's.

5. Keep the image of what your product can do for prospects illuminated clearly and brightly in your own mind.

6. Have a well-formed outcome, or plan, in mind. When an author writes a magazine article, she devotes close to eighty percent of her total time to writing the title and opening statement. Why? Because she realizes that she has only a few seconds to grab the reader's attention and interest. You have the same few seconds so plan them out.

7. Be prepared to provide the prospect with information before beginning to ask them questions. You can use a brief introduction, a summary of the events leading to the

meeting, a statement of common purpose or objective, and even a mention of possible benefits you are prepared to address.

8. Be prepared for anything to happen. Remember the "Law of Requisite Variety" and the adaptability of the chameleons? The more flexible you are, the more choices you have for successful outcomes.

Each of the points above represents an individual skill set for you to begin habituating and implementing into your set of existing sales skills.

While You Wait

Always carry work with you than can be done while you wait to see a prospect. Prospects have their own agenda, their own emergencies, and do not work on your schedule.

Carrying work with you can accomplish three important objectives:

1. It is a valuable time management tool that helps you gain valuable work time.

2. It keeps your anxiety level down and keeps you in a more positive mental focus.

3. And it does seem to make time pass faster.

Do not plan on using this waiting time to prepare for the call at hand. That preparation is to have been done the day before the call.

The Elements Of An Approach

The six major elements within the Approach Step are:

Sales Environment
Introduction

Rapport
Overview Statement
Benefit Idea
Transition Question

1. Sales Environment. Be observant of the prospect's environment, or of the environment into which you bring your prospects. Ask yourself this major question, "Is this environment contributing to, or distracting from, the total sales process?" Make as many adjustments in the environment as possible to make it a contributing factor to the sale.

2. Introduction. Never assume the correct pronunciation of the prospect's name and title, and never assume that the prospect remembers you or your company. Prepare an introduction and use it consistently. During my years of selling for the Burroughs Corporation, and as well known as Burroughs was in the banking industry, my memories are still clear of select bankers who would remember me after the first call as Jim Burroughs from The Robertson Corporation. It sounds strange, but it's true. We recently received some market research stating that a new prospect had to hear from you THREE TIMES before they even realized that you had been in communication with them. Three times, not once! Just think about that for a minute.

In our training we also continue to think it appropriate to express your appreciation for the prospect's taking time out of their schedule to talk with you; this is the time to express that appreciation.

3. Rapport. Developing rapport with the prospect is the basis for developing some level of a harmonious working relationship. Rapport can be established around common interests held between you and the prospect that are business related, or non-business related. Immediate rapport can be established by adjusting or "calibrating" to your prospect's behaviors, nonverbal signals, and words. Always be prepared to initiate the development of rapport,

although you will not always be able to initiate it. Some prospects will not want to do business with either you or your company. Experience and the careful practice of your observation skills will be an effective teacher of this technique.

4. Overview Statement. Be prepared to briefly tell the prospect the events that led to your meeting. This can be as brief as letting them know how you heard about them or their organization. You may want to briefly cover the steps you have taken in preparing for the meeting, but keep your statements brief and oriented to supporting their needs and wants, not yours.

5. Possible Benefits. During the Approach Step it is appropriate to at least give the prospect a hint into the possible benefit you might be to them. Do not move into the desire and conviction step of the sale. IBM salespeople are trained to just open the benefit box slightly and let the prospect begin to smell the roses. Introducing "possible" customer benefits too early in the sales cycle will only work to produce additional objections and questions from prospects. This is the time when you begin selling the prospect on why you even have the right to occupy their valuable time. Here you begin to answer the question of, "Why should I even listen to this person?" or "What's in this conversation for me?" Answer this question for yourself: "If the prospects does not need to be sold on why they should take valuable time our of their schedule to talk with you, then why didn't they call you in the first place?"

6. Transition Question. Be prepared to move out of the interest step and into the attention step of the sale as dictated by the prospect. One technique for accomplishing this is through a question.

EXAMPLE: You say, "Before talking about the types of benefits we can offer you as a training consultant firm, would you please tell me just a little bit about your needs for a more effective sales force?"

Where do you get the information that lets you know the type of transition question to use? Right again, during the preparation before the sale.

Why Prospects Do Not Become Customers

Following right along with the attention step of the sale, you can generally take all of the reasons prospects do not become customers and place them into five major categories:

NO NEED
NO WANT
NO VALUE
NO URGENCY
NO TRUST

TRUST is last on the list, but first with prospects. The typical salesperson will lose more prospects each year because they lack trust in that salesperson as a solution to their problems than for any other reason.

Do some discovery work on your own in this area.

- Go to your quiet spot.
- Begin your deep breathing routine. In for six . . . out for six . . . in for six . . . out for six.
- You are calm, quiet, and relaxed.
- Feel the beating of your heart. You are matching the rhythm of your breathing to your heart beat. You are calm, quiet, and relaxed.
- Slowly page back through your memory until you locate a business person you trust. Search until you can find their face. If you can visualize another salesperson that you trust implicitly, focus on them.

Focus on a face.

- You are with that person. Notice their features, eyes, mouth, hands. Notice the way they are dressed, how close they stand to you, the feeling in the air around you and the smells.
- Take in the total environment. You are the environment.
- You are talking with each other. Listen to the conversation, particularly the words you and the person use.
- You are calm, quiet, and relaxed.
- Consider again how you have grown to trust this person. Are they sincere? Are their actions congruent with what they say?
- You are quiet, and in their behavior you can sense some of the very reasons for your trust. You are relaxed and fully aware of how you feel trust in them.
- You are calm, quiet, and relaxed.

Record as many images as you can concerning why you developed trust in this particular individual. Be as vivid in your descriptions as possible.

Some features of the individual that communicated trust to me were:

_____

_____

_____

_____

I trust an individual when/because:

_____

_____

_____

_____

Others trust me because:

_____

_____

_____

_____

The traits you listed above will be some of the very same characteristics you will want to cultivate in order to develop a feeling of trust with your prospects.

You are in sales as a career and trust will become a vital element of your ability to sell on the other side of peak performance. Developing trust is a journey and not a destination. The task of developing and maintaining the trust of prospects and customers has a very slow beginning and never ends.

Attitudes Versus Behaviors

Once you have started your list of images, further divide it into two categories. One will be attitudes, the other behaviors. We have already talked about the importance of words. "Attitude" and "behavior" are two words that tend to get used a lot in sales training. Ask yourself one question, "How well do you really understand these two words?"

Take a quick test.

After each of the words that follow, please check off whether you think they are an attitude or a behavior.

WORD	Attitude	Behavior
1. Rude	_____	_____
2. Not at work on time	_____	_____
3. Not enthusiastic	_____	_____
4. Insubordinate	_____	_____

5. Makes a lot of errors   _____   _____

It may come as a big shock to find out that not one of those phrases or words is a behavior.

Learning a lesson about the difference between attitudes and behaviors came in the form of a hearing grievance over the termination suit of a saleswoman. The judge did a very interesting thing with the two managers involved in a hearing over the firing of this individual. During the proceedings, the judge asked both of the managers to independently write out their definitions of the five terms and phrases listed above. These five items were the major reasons listed on the saleswoman's termination document. It got even more interesting when the judge got the definitions, or lack thereof, from the managers. First of all, their definitions were not even close to being the same. One of the managers could not even define insubordinate and the other could not define enthusiasm.

You already know the end of the story. Management, and the company, lost. One of the managers, however, did a very intelligent thing. He apologized to the woman, wanted her to come back to work, and asked that she help him re-write her job description so that this sort of thing did not happen again.

What this manager learned was that an attitude is a feeling or emotion toward a fact or state. An attitude can even be a predisposition to act or not act in a predetermined manner. However, an attitude is not the act itself. The resulting behavior is the act. When you can see it, it becomes a behavior.

How clear is your sales job description? Is it written with attitudes, behaviors, or with accomplishments? For the benefit of all concerned it should be written in terms of behaviors and accomplishments that all parties have agreed upon.

Importance For The Attention Step In Sales

BEHAVIOR is a very important concept for sales and to the attention step of the sale. Years ago people studying psychology were convinced that attitudes drove behavior. This was pretty much the theory of the day until a man named Carl Rogers came along and said, "Guess what? Attitude is not the only driver of behavior, and not only that, but behavior can drive attitude." This was a new idea for salespeople.

What Carl Rogers was saying is that not only do you sing in the shower because you are happy, but singing in the shower can make you happy. Behavior does impact attitude. You do not only approach a prospect effectively because you have a positive attitude, you can develop a positive attitude by approaching a prospect effectively. Your behavior can, and does, impact your attitude.

This Is More Than A Technique Manual

While this book presents you with specific sales techniques to enhance your performance, it is more than just a sales technique manual.

Somewhere out there in the world sales trainers and sales managers are starting off their Monday morning sales meetings with a sales technique they picked up in a "new" book over the weekend.

1. Trainers arm their sales force with this new and improved version of an old technique.

2. The sales force proceeds to go out into the field and inflict this new technique upon unsuspecting prospects.

3. More often than not, the technique does not work, the prospects wonder what in the world is going on, the salespeople are embarrassed, and the technique goes by the

way, never to be seen again.

This is not an example of high performance selling. And it certainly is not fun for any of the parties involved.

Take one sales technique you are using currently and run it through the following set of questions:

Your sales technique is:_____

1. The purpose of this technique is:

_____

_____

_____

_____

2. The individual who benefits most from my using it is:

_____

_____

_____

_____

3. It fits into my overall strategy for selling because:

_____

_____

_____

_____

4. The skills involved in implementing the technique include:

_____

_____

_____

_____

5. I know that this technique has become a habit with me because:

_____

_____

———————————————————————————

———————————————————————————

There are two considerations with this technique.

A. If the answers to your questions are not in favor of the technique, consider replacing it with a more appropriate one. This may not be a valid technique for you to be habituating.

B. Should you determine the technique to be of value to the customer but not yet habituated or integrated into your selling, you can devote additional time to its effective implementation by placing it on a 21-day implementation plan.

Paying Compliments

One technique for getting a prospect's attention is to refine your skills in paying compliments.

During a sales training program for a major hotel in San Francisco, a participant asked about the damage done by using INSINCERE COMPLIMENTS. The answer to their question was that there is no such thing as an insincere compliment. It is either a compliment or it is not. Now don't get me wrong. Your prospect may decode or consider a compliment you gave them as being insincere, but there can be no question in your mind that your "purpose" was to help the prospect feel better about themselves. Your purpose was to show them a sign of respectful recognition. You were recognizing their individuality. You were truly paying them a compliment.

There is a corollary in NLP to "what you say" and "what you intend" by your compliment—and that is that the intention of what you say isn't what others perceive as your "meaning." The result you GET is your MEANING! This

principle is summarized succinctly in the following statement: *the meaning of your message is the response you get,
regardless of what you intend by your communication.*

These are the techniques involved in paying compliments:

1. Be mentally aware and habitually looking for the
good in both yourself and others. This will be easier for
those salespeople with high "Influencing" or "I" tendencies
(remember your prospect-watching categories) as they
tend to be optimistic and look for the good side of things.
So, get your "influencing" tendencies up! This is your
optimistic side and we all have at least some of this tendency. Let those tendencies get up there and go to work for
you when the situation calls for it!

2. Do not compliment the obvious. You will only be the
thousandth sales person to do so. Jack, a corporate buyer
with a major hospital, always kept a golf trophy on his desk.
When a new salesperson called on Jack, that salesperson
would invariably say something like, "Oh, you must be a
good golfer." Or, "I love to play golf. Do you play?" Jack took
great delight in responding, "I keep this on my desk as a
reminder that all salespeople do is play golf and compliment the obvious. Now, what was it you wanted?" It's cruel,
but Jack gets to the point.

3. Compliment a behavior. People are always a lot more
certain of their clothing than they are their behavior, so it
is their behavior they want to know about.

4. Tell them a little about how what you are com-
plimenting makes you feel. Let them know it makes you feel
good, or whatever your appropriate feeling is. This is the
emotional side of the coin versus the rational side.

5. Let them know the effect of their behavior. What
happens as a result of what they did? Is your day a little
brighter because of it? Then tell them.

Here is an example of paying compliments that we saw
in a bank where we were conducting a sales workshop. A

customer walked up to the bank teller. The teller did not look as if she was having a particularly nice day, but the customer had a very pleasing smile. The teller looked up at the lady and commented, "Thanks, I sure needed that smile. I feel better already and I've got to tell you, it sure makes the day go better."

1. Was that a compliment?
2. Did it meet all of the requirements?
3. How do you think it made the customer feel?
4. How do you think it made the teller feel?
5. Want to be effective in the attention step of the sale?

Start right now to become an effective compliment carrier.

Creating An Image For Attention

The last phase of this chapter is to determine how others develop trust in you as a salesperson. Remember, developing trust with prospects is a journey, not a destination.

- Go to your quiet spot.
- Begin your deep breathing routine. In for six . . . out for six . . . in for six . . . out for six.
- You are calm, quiet, and relaxed.
- Feel the beating of your heart. You are matching the pace of your breathing with your heart beat. You are calm, quiet, and relaxed.
- Slowly page back through your memory until you locate a client who has developed trust in you. If you are new to sales, locate the face of any individual who has developed that trust. Focus on that person.

You are with that person.
- Focus until you can see both yourself and the client in the same picture. Watch yourself as you enter the room. Watch your prospect.
- See or recall something about the prospect that you appreciate. Focus in on that.
- Watch and listen as you pay them a compliment.
- Notice their reaction. Notice yours. Process the image until it is clear. Make the image a black and white photo. Now make it color.
- Allow the image to flow and develop. Go with it. You are calm, quiet, and relaxed.
- Your images are enjoyable. Have fun with them.
- Now you are preparing to call on a new prospect. You have only met this person once before.
- You are entering their office. You are calm, quiet, and relaxed. Focus on the environment. You are the environment.
- Focus on their face and features.
- Now focus on your face and features.
- Process the entire room. Become the room. You are the room. You are the environment.
- All of your senses are working.
- You are mentally engaged and physically relaxed.
- Notice something that you appreciate about this individual.
- Focus on what it is that you appreciate.
- Listen as you pay them a compliment.
- Notice their reaction.
- Notice yours. Process the image until it is clear.
- Allow the image to flow. Go with it.
- You are calm, quiet, and relaxed.

Record Your Images

Take a minute and record some of your images.
I felt:

_____

_____

_____

_____

Most of my images were:

_____

_____

_____

_____

The behavior I complimented was:

_____

_____

_____

_____

The most important thing I learned from this experience was:

_____

_____

_____

_____

Take the attention getting techniques you have been
using and put them through the five step process presented
in this chapter. Use the ones that come out successfully and
seriously consider discarding the ones that do not.

Start New Habits Right Now
Do Not "Try" Stopping Old
Habits Tomorrow

7

The Doctor's Roadmap For Sales

Interest Step Of The Sale

SALES CYCLE   PROSPECT
                            BUYING CYCLE

SALES CYCLE	PROSPECT BUYING CYCLE
Approach • • • • • • • • • •	Attention ←
Fact Finding • • • • • • • • •	Interest ←
Presentation/Recommendation • • • •	Conviction ←
Handling Objections • • • • • • •	Desire ←
Closing the Sale • • • • • • • •	Action ←

The doctor was in the middle of an imagery session during a sales training program (that's right, we actually had a doctor attend a sales training program), and from the front of the room you could have seen a smile move completely across his face. Dr. G. had his eyes closed; he was physically relaxed yet mentally processing. Then, as if to communicate that he had completed the assignment, the smile left his face. He replaced it with a serious look and began moving his left foot up and down. The remainder of the group continued working through the exercise on imagery, but it was obvious that Dr. G. had mentally moved on to a new area. His eyes remained closed. He remained relaxed, but the doctor had made a shift.

The group was going through the same imagery exercise you went through to help image your purpose in sales. The discussion with the doctor that followed ended up telling the group more about the interest step of the sales process than how to write a statement of purpose.

As soon as the exercise was completed, we started with Dr. G. to find out what those images were all about. He said the first thing he imaged was a patient coming into his office. She had an expression of pain on her face and he went on to describe the other senses he used in determining that she was in pain. Then he began describing his inner feelings at the prospect of potentially being able to help this lady. This was the point in his exercise where the smile had crossed his face. He recalled their going through some light conversation and then the interesting implications for sales training began.

Once Dr. G. had established in his own mind that he had her attention and that some level of rapport was developing, he turned to a more analytical mode. This was when the smile left his face. His left foot had started to move, and his general mode shifted.

The doctor knew that he had her attention, and then moved on towards the prime objective for this step of the sale. That's right, doctors have a sale to make just as you do. Dr. G. made the shift and initiated the process of gathering information, fact-finding. Even with her medical history right in front of him, he gathered information and confirmed the old. You do the same in sales.

Dr. G. then asked a question that allow the patient to respond freely. There was nothing guided, nothing canned, but he did know the questions to be asked, and both the sequence and the manner in which to ask them. He was allowing her to talk, express herself, and describe her problem and symptoms in her own terms. That was the patient's greatest point of interest, her own problems.

In sales the concept of allowing the prospect to go first is called PSYCHOLOGICAL RECIPROCITY. It means that when you listen to a prospect first, they are morally and psychologically bound to listen to you in return.

Let the prospect talk first. Allowing prospects to talk is how you get people interested in you and what you will say. You demonstrate interest in the prospect and what they have to say.

Begin now to form images of yourself showing, through your behavior, interest in a prospect—not just talking to them, but becoming interested in them. Too many sales-people develop the ineffective habit of talking TO prospects and never get around to communicating and developing rapport WITH prospects.

In the past you may have been working to create interest by talking. We are suggesting you begin creating interest by asking appropriate questions, observing, and listening.

Interest Building

The purpose of this step in the sales process is to VERIFY prior prospect and business information, OBTAIN new information concerning the prospect's needs and wants, and begin to identify the prospect's DOMINANT BUYING MOTIVE (DBM). It is during this step where you begin to build the legitimacy for yourself, your product, your organization, and for the remainder of the sales process.

Other Professions Share These Same Techniques

It is vital for your success in sales for you to realize that ALL PROFESSIONALS, not just salespeople, use the techniques we are presenting. *Webster's New World Dictionary* defines the word professional as, "of, engaged in, or worthy of the high standards of, a profession." In sales you are the one that sets your standards. You, the individual, are worthy. The techniques you habituate are a direct reflection of the standards you establish and of your personal worth to the prospect.

Road Map For Your Sale

In addition to creating interest through gathering information, the doctor we described from our training program was initiating the development of his road map for the remainder of the sale. During this step in the process the doctor's mode of operation had grown more serious and turned towards obtaining factual information. You could see his mode change when this occurred during the exercise in class. In your 'DiSC' behavioral tendencies, you would say his "Steadiness" or "S" tendency had gone up. Dr. G. had turned his listening rheostat up, slowed his pace down, became very patient, "calibrated" to the needs of the prospect, and systematically began to accumulate the data necessary to draw a road map for his prescription/sale.

The Missing Step In Sales

As the doctor described the previous events, others in the group began relating back to either their own experience in sales, or to salespeople with whom they had prior experience. Chuck, a CPA, commented that this was the missing step in sales that bothered him most about the salespeople he had not appreciated in the past. They had not taken the time to find out, really find out, what his needs, wants, and beliefs were before they began making their "pitch."

In the next session with this same training group, Larry, an investment salesperson, provided us with an appropriate example of really determining a prospect's DOMINANT BUYING MOTIVE (DBM), in place of attempting to create one. Larry told the group that he had been attempting to "sell" to a particularly wealthy investor for the last year or so and was not having any success. He knew that Mr. Garrison invested in the market regularly, but Larry just could not get any of that investment business. Following the second session of the sales training program Larry realized that he was attempting to sell out of his own needs and wants base and that he knew nothing about the DBM of Mr. Garrison.

The very next day Larry decided to call Mr. Garrison and ask him how he was doing in the market. Here is part of that conversation after Larry had introduced himself.

Larry: ". . . and how have you been doing in the market the last quarter?"

Mr. G: "Pretty good. Did you call with some specific recommendations for me today?"

Larry: "We always have recommendations, but the real reason I called this morning was just to get your response to a couple of questions. Mind if I ask them?"

Mr. G: "No, ask away."

Larry: "Why do you invest in the market, really?"

Mr. G: "Well, obviously to make money."

Larry: "Fine. Now what do you do with that money once your stocks or bonds have earned it?"

Mr. G: "In the first place, I stay away from bonds in this market so don't even try talking to me about them; and in the second place when I decide to take my profit off a stock,

I sell it just like everyone else. Do you have a new way of doing all that?"

Larry: "Not really, but all that really leads me to the real question. What do you do with that money?"

Mr. G: "I put it in the bank."

Larry: "And then it does what?"

Mr. G: "Well, after the basics of our retirement are covered that is another question. Right now we are saving for a trip to China. I'm a golf nut and Arnold Palmer has just built what we hear is a great course in China, and Ruth and I are going over there to play it."

Larry: "That's great. Just how close to that objective are you?"

Mr. G: "Not all that close, but we are getting there."

Larry: "Mr. Garrison, I really appreciate your time and as soon as I have something that can get you closer to your China trip you will hear from me."

Mr. G: "I'll talk about that trip anytime, so give me a call."

After the telephone conversation what new information does Larry have?

1. Mr. Garrison's current Dominant Buying Motive (DBM) for investing is a golf trip to China.

2. Mr. Garrison's investment objectives are more cash than equity oriented.

3. Mr. Garrison likes to play golf.

4. Larry can talk with Mr. Garrison about any investment that will get him closer to the trip to China.

A very productive phone call!

The Number One Distinction Of Successful Salespeople

After making and observing literally thousands of sales calls, it has become obvious to me that a major distinction of successful salespeople is their ability to ask questions that determine the prospect's major reason, problem or need for taking action and then expand on that element. Effective salespeople do not invent the justification for the prospect to become a customer, they assist the prospect in uncovering and expanding upon value.

The Action Step Begins Here

The number one question we receive in our sales seminars is "How do I close a sale?" That turns into "When do I close?" and "Which technique do I use?" These questions actually move you further and further away from the center of your selling, the prospect. What we tell participants is that when you look at the entire process of closing a sale (we will be calling it the action step), a major element of the action process is initiated right here, during the interest step. An element of the action step begins here because this is where you begin formulating the prescription for solving the prospect's problem, and then moving prospects towards that solution or decision.

The model below illustrates how you actually begin formulating the prescription to a prospect's problem in the interest step of the sale and how these two steps work together.

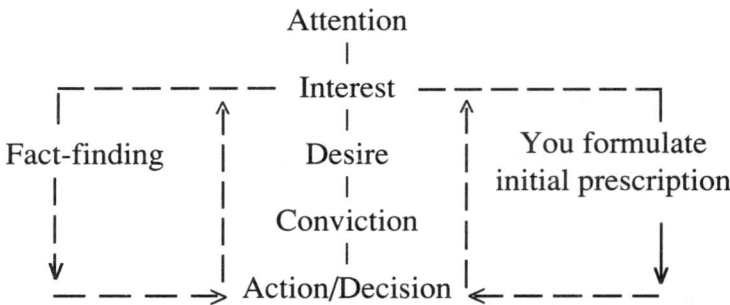

A Lesson From Sports

In 1976 Jack Nicklaus, famous golf professional, made an interesting observation that can impact the way you think about helping a prospect take action during the sales process.

When describing how he visualized a golf shot, Jack had traditionally commented that he saw himself set up to the golf ball, saw the golf swing, saw the flight of the ball, watched the ball land on the green and roll into the hole. In 1976 he commented that he had been describing the process in reverse. What actually happened was that he FIRST saw and determined the result he wanted to accomplish and then the imagery process REACTED to that goal or image. What Jack was doing was first seeing the golf ball go in the hole, visualizing its roll across the green, seeing the corresponding ball flight to produce that roll, then seeing the corresponding club swing to produce that flight, and finally he would move into the center of the process and react to the appropriate images. He was working from the desired result back to an appropriate reaction.

In sales you take the same course of action as Jack Nicklaus does in golf. During this step of the buying process you determine the appropriate solution(s) for the prospect and then you work backwards from that goal and react to it by designing the appropriate presentation. You are RE-ACTING to the prospect's problems, not ACTING upon your own needs and wants. You adapt to their perspective instead of trying to force your perspective upon them.

Your Doctor

Image this. You are in your doctor's office. The doctor greets you, comments on how awful you look, sits you down in one of those little rooms away from the entire world, and hands you a great big book. This is THE BIG BOOK! It has to be big. In this book are all of the diseases and ailments known to modern man. After giving you the book she politely asks you to read through the book until you find the ailment you think you have. Having accomplished that task, there is a cross-reference in the back that offers the correct solution to your particular ailment. What your doctor wants you to do is find the ailment you have and determine the appropriate cure. Then she will return and write out the prescription to cure it. Image your reaction in this situation!

Your reaction is probably quite obvious. If not, you may be less well off than suspected. A logical response would be to acknowledge the doctor's request, wait until she leaves the room, and then quietly, though quickly, run for your life to another doctor.

So why do you think the process in sales is any different than with an effective doctor? Far too many of the salespeople we observe on sales calls act far too much like the fictitious doctor just described. Yet these same salespeople still wonder why prospects do not call them professionals and do not TRUST them.

It is in this step of the buying process (Interest step)

that you determine, through listening, the needs, wants, and beliefs of your prospect. During this step, you work to determine the prospect's exact problem, translate it into several possible solutions, and begin to formulate a personalized prescription for that prospect.

During this step of the buying process is where the differences in your personal selling goals, individual styles, and sales markets really begin to show up.

In selling large communication switching systems for communication companies, their salespeople would typically invest many weeks and hundreds of hours in the information gathering phase of the sale. Yet even within the same company, the directory sales division (Yellow Page advertising) would spend far less time in this same step of the sale. In the directory division the action rate (they called it "closure") per day could be as high as six accounts. Someone selling major switching networks might sell only one system a month. There can be a significant difference in the amount of time and resources invested in this one step of the sales cycle.

In selling large computer systems many salespeople do very well and make only one sale a year. Much of that time difference is taken up right here, in the interest/fact-finding stage of the process.

Listen For Associated Feelings

Objectives:
1. Build interest and an appropriate focus within the prospect.
2. Gain sufficient information to define their major problem.
3. Expand on their problem, concern, or need.
4. Develop a tentative prescription for their problem.

To accomplish these objectives you need a lot of input from the prospect, and this means more than mere facts. Facts, by themselves, are like lightbulbs with no power flowing through them. The lightbulb is there, but without electricity there is no light. In sales, a prospect's emotions or feelings are the electricity for their lightbulb to action. To generate light you need both the light bulb and the electricity. To generate a decision in sales, you need to know both the facts of the situation and the prospect's associated feelings.

Even with all of the facts you still only have half the message. Until you know the related feelings, the lightbulb will not stay on. Assuming means giving yourself the ability to "mind read"—which can lead to problems in business! Assumptions are always dangerous in sales, and when you assume the feelings connected with an event the chances are great that you will miss the picture entirely. Mindreading can get you into trouble: observing and asking questions can help you understand your prospect more fully and lead you both toward your mutual goals.

FACT: A prospect already has a vendor for your product.

RELATED FEELING: They could be glad they have the vendor or they could be upset with the vendor. The associated feeling makes the difference.

FACT: They had a bad experience with your firm a few years ago.

RELATED FEELING: But that was a long time ago, there are no associated bad feelings now, and they will talk with you. OR they still hold a great deal of resentment and really want you out of their office and sight! Again, there may be a big difference based on the associated feelings.

Write out an associated fact for your own business situation that changes dramatically with the related feelings of the prospect.

FACT:

_____

_____

_____

_____

_____

_____

POSSIBLE RELATED FEELINGS:

_____

_____

_____

_____

_____

_____

_____

In listening for associated feelings, keep it simple. For each major discussion point search out one of the following appropriate core feelings:

GLAD
SAD
MAD
SCARED

Combine the feeling with the fact and the light will go on.

Open-Ended vs. Close-Ended Questions

Effective salespeople know to use open-ended and close-ended questions. Open-ended questions tend to be more effective and let's take a brief look at why.

OPEN-ENDED QUESTION. Example: What advantages accrue to the prospect when you, the salesperson, use open-ended questions?

CLOSE-ENDED QUESTION. Example: Do you use open-ended questions?

The advantage of open-ended questions in short sales cycles are many. The advantage to you, the salesperson, is that these questions allow and encourage your prospect to expand on their thoughts and feelings. This gives you the time and opportunity to tune in and really listen while they talk. Take the input from prospects and re-create a more complete image of what they are really seeing, hearing and feeling in the theater of their minds. It is said that if you listen long enough the prospect will tell you what you have to do to sell them. Open-ended questions are a technique that facilitate the listening process and prompt additional input from prospects.

The advantage of open-ended questions to the prospect is that it provides them with the opportunity to communicate to you their version of the situation at hand, their associated feelings, and in the end they will benefit from a more appropriate solution. Plus, and this is a big plus, the prospect is more apt to feel good about establishing a new business relationship and feel that is is a positive element for both themselves and their organization.

You Can Clarify Their Thinking— But Prospects Are Never Wrong

On many occasions you will be listening to a prospect, and the more they vocalize their thoughts and feelings, the better perspective they create in their own mind concerning what they really do need or want. This is another benefit of open-ended questions. Sometimes prospects really are just "looking around." By allowing prospects to talk, they will often bring out needs and wants that have never surfaced before. Talking is itself great therapy for the prospect.

If You Could Only Image What I Image

During a sales seminar he conducted for a firm I was with, Mr. Zig Ziglar, perhaps the best known sales speaker of our time, said that "90% of selling was a transfer of feelings." That statement paints a pretty clear picture, and I would never say that Zig was wrong, but my view is that the sales horizon can be extended past feelings alone.

Since we think and process information in the form of images, Zig might have said that "90% of selling was a transfer of images." Remember, images incorporate all of the senses—taste, sight, hearing, touch, sounds, and feelings. At this stage of the sale, prospects are formulating their images and associated feelings of you, your organization, your product, and your facilities.

Service After The Sale

Let's look at (or image) an example of what we are talking about in terms of images and feelings. Think for a minute about your representing an offering where your customers place a large amount of emphasis on service after the sale. Image yourself as being well into the sales call when the prospect asks, "Just how good is your service?" Before you answer their question, what would it be helpful for you to know? Right, it would be helpful for you to understand their definition of the term "good" service. Consider that you really do NOT know the prospect's image or definition of "good" service until they have painted the picture for you. What does the term "good" really mean to your prospect? Their images are important, not yours!

High Need Tendencies:	"Good" could emphasize:
Dominance/"D"	-Fast and they can control it
Influencing/"I"	-Friendly and lots of contact
Systematic/"S"	-Systematic and orderly
Compliance/"C"	-Perfect and meets all standards

Use open-ended questions to help your prospect communicate more accurately their realities and expectations of you, your offerings, and your service.

Getting Started

It is early in the fourth quarter of the football game and the Washington Redskins have been leading the Dallas Cowboys for the entire game. The Redskins are driving and are down to the twenty yard line. At that moment the Cowboys intercept a pass and run it back ninety yards for a touchdown. Dallas goes on to score two more touchdowns late in the fourth quarter and beat Washington by three points (an actual game).

What happened? The TV commentator reflects back to the interception and says that the interception changed the MOMENTUM of the game from Washington to Dallas. Momentum is certainly an important element in sales as well. QUESTION: If the momentum in sales can change, how do you get it started your way in the first place?

In football they begin the game with a kickoff. In sales you do the same, only you do not use a football, you use questions.

Here is an example.

Salesperson: May I ask you a quick question? (I know; that is a close-ended question, but I use it a lot and it has one real advantage— it works!)

Prospect: Certainly.

Salesperson: What are a few of the things you like best about the _____ (you have to fill this in with the offering they are using) you are using currently? (Now an open-ended question.)

In reality, most of you are selling to prospects who already use products and/or services that have some similarity to yours. You realize how unique your offering is but prospects may not. The two questions used above accomplish several things for both you and the prospect.

1. The prospect starts talking.

2. As the prospect describes the positive aspects of what they are currently using, it gives you an idea of the basics you must meet to remain competitive.

3. The discussion begins on a positive note.

4. You are reminded to NEVER knock the competition. NEVER.

5. The prospect gives you a loyalty reading. If they begin "selling" you on the merits of what they are using, there is a lot of momentum to turn around. If their list is short, and they even begin beating up the product or service, you have less momentum to overcome.

6. You can listen for feelings as well as content/facts.

Next Question Please

Salesperson: Can I ask another quick question?
Prospect: Certainly. (They always say certainly, at least in my images.)
Salesperson: If there was one thing you would change about _____ (you have to fill this in with what they are using), what might it be?

This technique accomplishes several objectives for both you and the prospect.

1. You get another loyalty reading.

2. Prospects can knock the competition, but you do not join in.

3. You can determine additional feelings as well as content.

4. As prospects discuss these points, it gives you the input you need on areas where you can excel. This is your opening.

Do not remain in this step of the sales process too long or you will become a professional visitor. "Too long" is another relative sales term that you will learn about from experience.

You Are Ready To Journey On To The Next Stage

8

They Take Them Out Into The Bush Country And The Animals Eat Them

Desire And Conviction Steps Of The Sale

SALES CYCLE   PROSPECT
                               BUYING CYCLE

During a sales seminar for a group selling retirement communities in Florida, one of the salespeople provided a great lead into a sales presentation. Judy related to the group that she had really worked on a presentation to be given to a group of retirement age members of a local church. The average age of the audience was seventy. Even with all of her preparation she got up to address the group and went totally blank. Not a word of her presentation would come to her. The only images that flew through her memory were of her past years of missionary work in Africa. Judy played back these images, faced the group directly and announced, "In the villages where I worked in Africa, when the old people ceased to be productive, the villagers no longer considered them as functioning members of the tribe so they took them out into the bush country and let the wild animals eat them. BOY, DO WE HAVE A BETTER PLAN FOR YOU THAN THAT!"

Judy got the group's attention for the remainder of her presentation.

Desire And Conviction

The purpose of this step of the buying process is to present your prescription for your prospect's problems and to present yourself, your product, and your organization in an organized and convincing fashion. In this step of the sale you prove in the legitimacy of what you can accomplish for the prospect and that you can meet their DOMINANT BUYING MOTIVE (DBM). Proving in legitimacy and value is the conviction part of the process and meeting their DBM is the desire element.

Where Is Your Prospect Right Now?

By this stage in the sales process you have:

1. Gained the prospect's attention with your approach. You also initiated the development of rapport between you and the prospect.

2. Prepared them to listen and appreciate you by your

listening to, and showing respect for, them first.

3. Used observing, listening and questioning techniques to develop a preliminary estimate of their needs and wants, and formulated an initial prescription for their problem. You have identified their preferred mode for processing, storing, and retrieving information—visual, auditory or kinesthetic. You know what is important to them in their decision-making process.You have them ready to listen to you and their ears are open. But what about their minds? LISTENING and HEARING are two very different things.

Image this definition of desire: "An emotion or stimulation process of the mind, directed to the attainment or possession of an object from which pleasure is expected; a wish, craving, or longing to obtain or enjoy."

In addition to being ready to listen, you want prospects DESIROUS of what you are offering.

Creating Desire

Desire is stimulated within prospects through statements and images/sounds/feelings of satisfaction, not from being asked questions by the salesperson. Select your most effective words and let the prospect discover what your offering holds for them. Let them see, hear and feel what it will mean to them and to their companies to go along with you and your prescription.

To be effective, your desire producing statement must:

1. Be a statement, not a question.

2. Have a direct impact on their major needs, wants, or related problems of concern.

3. Get them saying, either to themselves or to you, "prove it!"

4. Be supported, or at least supportable, by evidence.

5. Include emotion (intuition and "gut feeling") as well as logic when appropriate.

The Prospect Took Over

Once, while doing a particularly average job of selling, a prospect actually ended up making the following statement for one of our salespeople. The sale was to the point where optimally the salesperson would have been orchestrating the desire step of the sale, but they dropped the baton and the prospect had to take over. The salesperson was visiting, not selling. They were right in the middle of a casual conversation when the general manager of the conference center looked at the salesperson and said something like, "You know, Gary told me some nice things about what your leadership training program accomplished for his center in Dallas, but that was not what really impressed him. He said that the skills he learned in the program did more for his relationship with his wife and family than anything he had ever experienced. How could that be true of a leadership program for conference center managers?"

All that remained was for the salesperson to present enough appropriate evidence to enable the prospect to CONVINCE HIMSELF that his own claim was true and another prospect would become a customer. Since not all of your prospects will be as helpful as the one above, you need to start developing your own statements and claims right now.

Creating Your Own Statements

- Go to your quiet place.

- You are calm, quiet, and relaxed.
- You are breathing easily.
- Review the major characteristics for creating your statement. To be effective it will:
  1. Be a statement.
  2. Relate directly to a prospect's needs.
  3. Have prospects asking you to prove it.
  4. Be supportable by evidence.
  5. Include emotion directed toward a prospect's behavioral motivation.
- Write out your statement.
- With imagery, practice your delivery to specific prospects.
- Image their reactions.
- Refine the statement if necessary and continue practicing.

My initial statement is:

_____

_____

_____

_____

During imagery, I discovered that my statement could be improved with:

_____

_____

_____

My revised statement is:

_____

_____

_____

_____

Emotion Takes Prospects To A Decision— Logic Keeps Them There

When desire and logic begin a debate, desire typically wins out. While desire will motivate your prospect to action, it is logic that keeps them as CUSTOMERS, NOT CANCELLATIONS. "Buyer's remorse" has caused many a customer to break a sales contract. When the cold gray dawn of reality causes a customer to cancel a sale, it happens for the most part because the salesperson did not provide them with enough LOGICAL information to keep them convinced. Effective selling takes both logic and emotion—functions which, in current models of the brain, are specialized in opposite hemispheres! The balance of both is key.

Buyer's remorse is your fault. That's right.

YOU lead the prospect to buy on emotion.
YOU thought the sale would last forever.
YOU did not provide the necessary balance of logic.
BUYER'S REMORSE took over.
YOU caused it!

Therefore, even when prospects have already bought on emotion, be certain that you provide enough logic to keep the decision in your favor. In selling large ticket items, we have learned that many sales actually begin with the installation of the product, not with the signing of a contract.

The Interview

During the presentation is where you "mix" the necessary amounts of emotion with required parts of logic and produce the desired reaction with the prospect. That is why we call it the Desire & Conviction Step of the sale. You already know the decision that is best for your prospect. You determined that in preparation and confirmed it in fact-finding. Now is when prospects begin convincing themselves of the better decision, and of the value in that decision.

One "truth" about presentations is:

To be effective in sales
you must develop a
CANNED PRESENTATION.

You walk into a prospect's office and a tape recording comes on saying, "Kelly is not in right now. At the end of this message you will hear a tone. At the sound of the tone a video tape unit will come on and you have five minutes to leave your sales message." When that tone sounds you will be prepared.

Sales books are filled with advice on researching, writing, and delivering canned sales presentations, so that information is not duplicated here. You only need to remember one rule for delivering canned presentations to prospects.

RULE #1
You cannot deliver a canned presentation.

Effective preparation for sales requires that you research, write, and fully prepare to deliver a canned presentation. THIS PREPARATION IS FOR YOU, your sales manager and company, but not to deliver to your prospect. Effective selling demands that you have the flexibility to adapt to the prospect and the environment. In effective sales you react, not act. You are relaxed, resourceful, and have choices of action. You are reacting to the prospect's situation, not acting according to your own.

You can master a canned presentation but you can never deliver it to a prospect.

Deedee Lasker's Story

Deedee Lasker is a very fine golfer on the LPGA tour. The U.S. Golf Association allows her to carry fourteen golf clubs with her when she plays in a golf tournament. Deedee is very proficient in using each and every club, from her driver down to her putter. Her driver is the club she uses when she wants to drive a golf ball as far as possible. Her putter is for close shots on the green. Each club between her driver and putter has a specific function and distance it is used for.

Here are the major points you can learn from a professional like Deedee that transfer directly to your sales presentations:

1. VARIETY AMONG PROSPECTS IS INFINITE. Deedee knows that because of an infinite number of factors, no two golf shots are ever exactly the same. There are literally hundreds of variables with each shot. The same is true of selling. Therefore, Deedee approaches each shot as being unique and requiring individual attention and intention.

2. BECOME PROFICIENT WITH EACH QUESTIONING AND PRESENTATION TECHNIQUE BEFORE ATTEMPTING TO COMBINE IT WITH OTHERS AND USE IT TO HELP A PROSPECT.

In one year, Deedee may hit as many as forty thousand golf shots. Because each shot in a tournament is unique, there is no way she can prepare for each specific shot. She must develop a general proficiency for using each of her fourteen clubs BEFORE she attempts to adapt to individual shots. She practices the basics of each shot and technique in order to adapt to the specifics.

3. EACH PRESENTATION AND QUESTIONING TECHNIQUE HAS A SPECIFIC FUNCTION.

Each golf club was designed to create a specific reaction when it strikes the ball. A nine iron was designed to propel the ball high into the air; a one iron was not. A sand wedge was designed to move a ball out of sand; a putter was not. Deedee must learn the design functions, capabilities, and limitations of each golf club, and act accordingly. You will do the same with the techniques in your sales bag.

4. NOT ALL PROSPECTS REQUIRE A FULL PRESENTATION.

When Deedee needs to hit the ball a long distance, she uses her driver. When the ball is on the green, she uses her putter. She does not use her driver on a two foot shot. Do not give your full presentation to a prospect who only needs and wants a limited amount of information. Learn when to present, when not to present, and how much to present.

5. PROSPECTS AND THE ENVIRONMENT DICTATE THE ORDER, CONTENT, EMPHASIS, AND LENGTH OF YOUR PRESENTATION.

Deedee processes the total environment of the golf course and allows that information to dictate which club to use and how to use it. She receives all of her information from the target and environment, then reacts to that information. Her shot is only as good as the information she has processed and used. The same is true in sales, only you typically do not refer to prospects as "targets." The key in reacting is to remain in control, but not in obvious control, of the prospect. Effective selling is a reaction sport!

6. KEEP PROSPECTS INVOLVED AND ACTIVE.

Plan ways into your questions and presentations that keep your prospects actively, not passively, involved. Do not allow participation to happen by chance; plan it. Deedee does not BLOCK OUT any of the information or input available to her; she keeps all of the elements active and involved. Observe your prospects. Find out what makes them excited, passionate, and attentive, and find ways to work these elements into your presentations. This is not only at a subconscious level. You want it at a conscious level as well where you have choices available to you.

Our thanks go out to Deedee for the sales lesson.

Emotion And Logic

In learning the BALANCE between emotion and logic in your sales presentations, experience is your best instructor. Some presentations will be 80% emotional and 20% logical. Others will be just the opposite, and then there will be everything in between. The balance depends entirely on who? Right again, your prospect. Mixing this balance for individual prospects is a skill you will acquire over time as you grow from your experience.

Creating The Presentation—
Element By Element

When you take up the game of golf, you will want fourteen of the finest clubs in the world in your golf bag. However, you can still only use one club at a time. The particular golf club you use for each shot, the timing of the shot, and the total sequence of all the shots hit is a skill developed over time. The same is true with the elements and techniques of your sales presentations. First you develop your skill with the individual elements or techniques as you learn to combine them within the process.

A Way To Develop Elements Of Your Presentation

Among books there are different groupings—novels, fiction, etc. In developing units of desire and conviction for your sales presentations, distinct groupings exist also. One way to label these groupings is:

    1. Feature   3. Benefit
    2. Function   4. Verification

Here is one way (not the only way) to develop your sales presentations .

1. List the major FEATURES of your offering. Features are the qualities, attributes, and "things" prospects can touch and see about your product. These are the LOGICAL components. If there are not at least five features that set your product apart from your competition, consider quitting and go to work for them.

2. For each feature, list as many PROBLEMS it solves as you can. Revising your list will be an ongoing process as you and your customers will continually come up with new and more creative applications. For developing your original presentation, you should be able to come up with a minimum of three problem solutions for each feature. These can have either logical or emotional implications.

3. For each feature, develop at least three possible BENEFITS to prospects. Benefits are the values your prospects can receive from using and owning your product. These are emotional components. You know that a feature is only a benefit once your product is being used, but for right now go ahead and list possible benefits.

4. Be certain that you can VERIFY/PROVE statements you are going to use. Remember, following each statement in your presentation, the prospect's response should be,

"Great, prove it." If you say it, be certain you can prove it. This is a necessary logic component.

    5. Now, practice presenting all four elements in a single unit. YOUR OFFERING IS:_____

    UNITS OF DESIRE AND CONVICTION
    Example:
    1. THE FEATURE IS: Air conditioning in a new car.
      A. THE FUNCTIONS ARE: Lowers the temperature within your automobile by a certain number of degrees in a certain number of minutes.
      B. PROBLEM SOLVED: Profuse sweating.
      C. POSSIBLE BENEFITS ARE: Keeps your new business suit dry while driving to work when it is 1O4 degrees outside.
      D. YOUR VERIFICATION IS: Product literature on the cooling capacity of the unit, or personal experience.

Now work through your own examples.

    1. The feature is:_____
    A. The functions are:

_____
_____
_____

    B. Problems solved are:

_____
_____
_____

    C. Possible benefits are:

_____
_____
_____

D. Your verification is:

_____

_____

_____

2. The feature is:_____

A. The functions are:

_____

_____

_____

B. Problems solved are:

_____

_____

_____

C. Possible benefits are:

_____

_____

_____

D. Your verification is:

_____

_____

_____

3. The feature is:_____

A. The functions are:

_____

_____

_____

B. Problems solved are:

_____

_____

_____

C. Possible benefits are:

_____

_____

_____

D. Your verification is:

_____

_____

_____

The Flow Of The Presentation

While conducting a sales training program for a banking group, one individual new to sales commented that they still had difficulty developing the flow or rhythm for their presentation. Their question was, "How can I connect all of the information, the features, the problems solved, and the benefits surrounding a given banking service in a logical sequence that still flows?" These are the types of questions you love to get because they flow right into the sales program. To answer this question, we provide the participants in our programs with an adaptation of a technique first introduced to us by Mr. Lee DuBois, a well known sales trainer and trainer of trainers.

The following format can be very effective in presenting information for your prospect's consideration once you have determined their dominant buying motives (DBM) and developed your prescriptions or situations to their problems. In helping your prospect make an appropriate buying decision, it is important that you use this format only AFTER you have allowed them to advance through the Interest and Attention steps of the buying cycle.

UNITS OF VALUE. The following is an adaptation of the technique for presenting major customer benefits within the Desire & Conviction Step of the buying cycle that was taught to us in a sales training program conducted by Lee DuBois.

STEPS

1. YOUR MAJOR CLAIMS.
This step begins with the words, "We can provide . . . " or "You can . . ."
2. FACTS AND EVIDENCE IN SUPPORT OF YOUR CLAIMS. This step begins with the word, "Because . ."
3. SPECIFIC PROBLEMS SOLVED FROM USING YOUR OFFERING. This step begins with the words, "Which means to you . . ."
4. THE BUYER BENEFIT: YOUR PROSPECT'S DBM. Begin this step with the words, "And the real benefit to you is . . . ." In practice, this model looks something like the following:

A Major Claim . . . . . Susan, "you can" increase your sales for the coming year by over 20% as a result of having effectively implemented the techniques you can gain from our new peak performance training program;

Facts and Evidence . . . "because" you will learn the power of combining time tested and powerful sales techniques with the principles of peak performance learned from some of the world's greatest salespeople and professional athletes;

Problem Solved . . . "which means to you"
that you can help guide your
prospects towards making better
and faster buying decisions ;

DBM . . . . "and the real benefit to you will be"
that you will be able to sell more ef-
fectively, reach your true potential
in sales, and gain an even greater
sense of satisfaction from your
sales career.

Now is the time to create your own example.

The product or service is: _____
1. Your Major Claim. (Your statement about your offering that gets your prospect, even if to himself, to ask, "Can
you prove that?"
You can/we can provide:

_____
_____
_____
_____

2. Facts and Evidence. (The logical, factual information that backs up your original statement.)
Because:

_____
_____
_____

3. Specific Problem Solved. (Usually logical, not emotional, and gets them into ownership.)

_____
_____
_____

Which means to you:

_____

_____

_____

4. The specific benefit to the buyer. (The DBM.)
And the real benefit to you is:

_____

_____

_____

Rules For Practice

- 1. Use imagery to create a variety of situations and prospects with which to practice. Yes, this is the same as experience! The mind cannot differentiate between a "created" scenario and a memory of an actual experience; this is why mental imagery and visualization are so effective in achieving peak performance.
- 2. You do not have to use ALL four elements of each unit every time, you only need to be prepared to do so.
- 3. Go through each unit once emphasizing emotion.
- 4. Go through them again with heavy logical emphasis.
- 5. Practice BALANCING the emotion and logic in each unit.
- 6. Being able to adapt your presentation to each prospect will be your key to success; begin now.
- 7. Present the elements of each unit in reverse order. Give the verification first, then tell what those facts mean in terms of benefit to the prospect,

work the benefits into the functions, and finally let the prospect know the feature providing all of these benefits.

- 8. Be creative with your imagery! Make your scenario big, small, unfocused, wavy, sparkly, or two-dimensional. Vary the colors or make them black and white. Change your image from a still photo to a movie. Put a simple border around it or an antique picture frame. Make it tall and narrow or short and wide.

- 9. HAVE FUN WITH THIS DRILL. YOU WILL BE DEVOTING A LOT OF TIME TO PRACTICE AND IT MIGHT AS WELL BE FUN. REMEMBER, BALANCE IN YOUR PRESENTATIONS CANNOT BE TAUGHT BUT IT CAN BE LEARNED.

There are many techniques a sales instructor can teach you, but performing at peak levels means that you learn how to adapt your presentations to your prospects, and this type of experience base comes primarily through trial and error. Therefore, remember that trials and errors are only a function of the learning process.

Strive to be creative. Learn to be creative; it is a skill. Peak performance in sales lives and prospers in a world of creativity. Take one sales technique and use it in as many different situations, with as many different prospects, as possible. Learn to use it early in the call, late in the call, with a demanding prospect, with a friendly prospect. BE CREATIVE. Take that one technique and work with it through all four patterns of your "DiSC" profiling skills. Take one of your feature/function/benefit/verification sequences and implement it the same way. Give it 21 days. Invest just 21 days and you have a new habit!

A Final Note From Doug

In talking with Doug, a very successful real estate salesperson, about selling and sales techniques, he made a very interesting observation. He said that one of his sales objectives was to develop clients into "branch offices" for both himself and for his company. This was nothing new for the sales industry and is vital for generating both repeat business and word-of-mouth advertising. But then Doug added a question worth your consideration. His question was: "In many instances, doesn't the most important part of the sales cycle take place while you are actually AWAY FROM, versus when you are WITH, the prospect?"

Doug was absolutely correct and his question needs to impact the way you sell in two major ways:

1. Design your sales presentation and followup so that prospects can sell to others without you being present.

2. Remain in contact with your existing customer base to ensure that they remain "branch offices" for you and your organization.

Remember That Your Journey
To Top Sales Performance
Is Through Creativity

9

They Removed The Road Signs

Answering Objections, Concerns, And Questions

SALES CYCLE   PROSPECT
                               BUYING CYCLE

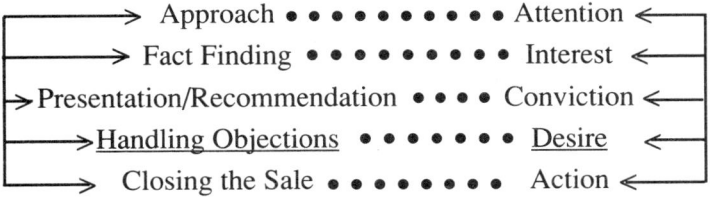

Mentally climb back into your car and prepare for another trip. In a few minutes, you will be traveling through some of the most spectacular high mountain country in the world. You will be driving West on Highway 22 out of Jackson, Wyoming, and into the Teton Mountain Range. Your car's motor is running, its top is down, your seat belt is fastened, and you are on your way. You are poised and fully engaged with the task at hand.

All your senses tell you that spring has come to the Tetons. The hillsides have turned into a tapestry of green.

Shades of green surround the countryside. You cannot help but notice the different shades of green. Look deep into the middle of that large pine over on your left. The middle of the pine is such a dark green that it looks almost black. You can smell the sharp pine and sage. Take a minute to fill in all the sensory details of your picture.

Your car's top is down. You hear the wind passing gently overhead and the sound is very calming. You are calm, quiet, and relaxed. You are at the top of the mountain. What a great view of the world below.

Begin your descent down the mountain road. You are into the first curve. The wind passing overhead becomes louder and louder. It is no longer calming to your senses but warns of something to come. You no longer look from side to side as your full attention becomes focused on the task at hand, getting down the mountain road safely. First your grip tightens, then your arms; now the tightness moves into your shoulders. Feel your muscles tighten. You experience difficulty holding onto the steering wheel and maintaining control. You have driven into the second curve at too high a rate of speed. There had been no warning of either the curve or the steep grade. There were no road signs. Your hands continue to tighten around the steering wheel. Your breathing becomes short and labored. Your heart rate quickens. The palms of your hands begin to sweat.

You finally steer through the last curve, move onto straight road, and are back in control. All of your senses give a sigh of relief. You are under control and moving safely down the mountain.

What happened? How did you get into difficulty in the first place? Think about it before going on.

Answering Questions And Concerns

The purpose of this step in the sales cycle is to get the sales process back on track when prospects begin to move away with questions, objections, concerns, rejections, stalls, or when they use that great word, "No!"

Effectively processing a prospect's questions assists you in determining where they are in the buying cycle. Who cares where you are in the sales cycle? The emphasis has to be on the prospect's buying cycle.

Objections are also an indication that you did not do a complete job of identifying and expanding the major problems or concerns of the prospect, or that you presented benefits too early in their buying cycle. Consider the possibility that 80% of all objections are caused by salespeople, not by prospects. Also consider that effective prospect qualification, needs verification and problem identification, and development of relative value to the prospect can eliminate 80% of all objections.

Road Signs

You got into difficulty while mentally driving down the hill because there were no road signs to warn you of the impending danger. Go back through your mental images if necessary and notice the absence of signs. You had taken road signs for granted; they were always there before.

"Objections" (we are going to call them "Questions from Prospects") are your road signs throughout the sales process. You will be less effective in sales when you lack information, direction, and feedback from the prospect. Effective selling requires a constant stream of feedback. Questions from the prospect are a major element of that feedback.

SALESPEOPLE LIVE
AND SURVIVE
ON FEEDBACK

Your anxiety in driving down the mountain resulted from the absence of signs. The same applies to prospects. The questions prospects raise are not good or bad, they just are. Questions are the road signs and cues that you need to help direct prospects to an appropriate decision and onto the right road to travel.

Masks And Coding

Emil, a successful sales trainer and retailer, says, "Selling does not begin until the questions begin, and without questions there would be no salespeople, only order takers." What Emil had learned through his years of experience in retail sales was that prospects become very effective at masking and coding their thoughts and feelings. It is only through effective questioning that you can begin to process through their misleading masks and codes. What you say and what they understand can be two entirely different things!

To help you sort through the masks and codes, we have worked out a basic classification of objections for you.

CLASSIFICATIONS/WHAT PROSPECTS ARE REALLY TELLING YOU:

Classification 1 - REJECTIONS
WHAT PROSPECTS ARE REALLY TELLING YOU:
"I do not like you, or your company or your offering. I am turning you away." (Spoken like a true 'D'.)

Classification 2 - BARRIERS AND STALLS
WHAT PROSPECTS ARE REALLY TELLING YOU:
"I need more time to think this over. (Spoken like a true 'C'.) I do not KNOW enough, or feel good enough, about you and your offering to make a decision at this time."

Classification 3 - QUESTIONS
WHAT PROSPECTS ARE REALLY TELLING YOU:
"Tell me more about your offering. I need more information." Could be a high 'S'. Check it out!

Classification 4 - OBJECTIONS
WHAT PROSPECTS ARE REALLY TELLING YOU:
"I know enough and I still am not not interested. There are some elements of your offering that I am in opposition to."

Classification 5 - JUSTIFICATION
WHAT PROSPECTS ARE REALLY TELLING YOU:
A reason you can accept as justification for their not going forward right now. And, what they have right now fits their needs and wants better than your offering.

By first determining the classification your prospect's mask or internal dialogue fits into, you can then select the appropriate way to help them move forward with some decision or level of commitment. You may discover that you have not done an effective job of qualifying the prospect in the first place and that you really do not have a prospect.

Turning Objections Into Questions

The Random House Dictionary tells you that an objection is: "a comment or reason offered in opposition, refusal, or disapproval." On the other side of that coin there is a question. The dictionary defines a question as: "something asked in order to get information, or a problem for discussion." The ball is back on your side of the court. Which would you rather have, a reason offered in opposition, or something asked in order to get information?

It Works

In selling their retirement living projects, one group of salespeople told me that they were receiving the same objection/question time and time again. They heard "but I'm just not ready" from prospects day after day. We were finishing some training work with a member of the sales group from the retirement center when a couple came into Jerry's (one of the salespeople) office and presented us with a very interesting training opportunity. Put your image machine and skills to work and form your own vision of the couple who came into Jerry's office. The man, being helped to a chair by his wife, was seventy-six years of age. The lady, then needing help from one of us after expending all of her energy getting her husband seated, was seventy-three years of age. They both had difficulty seeing, moving about, and had to be driven there by their daughter.

If anyone really needed the services this retirement community had to offer, they looked like the ideal prospect. They were ready!

The sales call went well until after the desire and conviction step. The couple looked at each other, then the lady stated, "Well, what you have to offer is very nice, but we just are not ready." Not only did she say it, it sounded like she meant it. If there ever was a ready couple, they were it. Opportunity seldom knocks twice (there is an interesting image to think about) and this seemed like a golden opportunity to test theory against reality. Diving right in, the salesperson said to the lady, "May I ask you a question?". . . She acknowledged and said yes. Here is the remainder of that dialogue.

He: "Are you satisfied that the safety features and room design will provide you with the security you are after?"

Her: "Yes."

He: "Are you confident that the dining facilities and food will provide the levels of nutrition you need for continued good health?"

Her: "Oh, yes." And she became very quiet again.

He: (after a pause) "Then, what is your question?"

Her: "Well, as I told you, we just are not ready to give up our home yet."

He: "So, the real question is, what type of major event, such as an accident or other problem, must happen before you are willing to accept a retirement community life style? Is that the question?" (Somewhat dangerous; but remember, he had the prospect's best interest firmly in mind.)

Her: (after another long pause) "No, the real question is getting up enough nerve to do what we know needs to be done. You see, we know this will be our last move, and that is difficult for folks like us to admit to ourselves. You just do not know what we are going through. Once we move in here, as nice as your facility is, we know that we will never leave."

She finally got down to the REAL QUESTION. Not an objection, but the question that was on the prospect's mind. In reality, the question had little to do with where the couple was GOING, and had everything to do with what they were LEAVING.

You will cover the remainder of the technique for

answering questions in the next chapter, but it is important that you process exactly what occurred in this situation before going on. This is an example of a technique that applies directly to selling at peak levels of performance because it helps the prospect clarify their own thinking about their needs and/or beliefs. It takes the focus away from you and it is effective in getting the prospect closer to making a reality-based decision.

You also receive benefit from using this type of questioning because you can determine where the prospects are in their decision-making process while they provide you with additional verbal and nonverbal information with which to work.

So The Real Question Is . . .

When you begin using the technique, use those exact words to open your first sentence. "May I ask you a question?" And make sure your voice has a real question mark in it.

When you ask that final, "So, the real question is," a couple of things are apt to happen. First, prospects actually begin changing the words they use. They begin including the word "question" in their statements. "Well, I guess my question is . . . " or, "It really is a question of . . .". This is your sign that their perception is changing. Now, you can work with them to get the question answered. Eight times out of ten they have the answer themselves. You just helped them get to it.

Another thing that is apt to happen when you start using the technique is that 80% of the time your question is NOT the right one at all. Some of the time you will not even be close. Do not worry. When you get prospects to this point in the sale effectively, they will tell you what the real question is. Either way, both you and the prospect win because now you know their real question.

Build Your Sales Bridge Of Value
A Little Wider

Now you have turned a prospect's objection into a question, so where do you go from here? Let's go back through the technique.

May I ask you a question? (Say yes.) Thank you.

How wide do you build the bridge of value? Answer: As wide as necessary.

Remember, when your prospects raise a question they are not saying "no," they are attempting to communicate to you that they do not "know" enough to give you their large amount of money to walk across your little bridge of value.

Let's review. In the Conviction and Desire step of the sale, you began constructing a bridge with your units of value and desire. At that point in the sales cycle, you were not certain of how long or how wide the bridge would have to be. You had an idea from preparation and the attention and interest steps, but you were not certain yet. By listening to the prospect's questions you can better determine just how high and wide your sales bridge to action has to be. So, go back into the Conviction and Desire step of the sale and CONSTRUCT ANOTHER UNIT OF VALUE for your bridge.

Trial and error is again a valuable teacher in this building process. This is yet another technique for helping the prospect that can be learned but is difficult to teach.

Flash Back

When the prospect's question requires additional information before you can continue building their bridge of conviction, where do you go in the steps of the sale?

Right! You go clear back to your interest building techniques. The Bible (which is a very good sales training book) even says that a person who attempts to answer a question before they understand it is a fool. You may have to go clear back to the interest building step of the sale when you do not understand their question.

Thank You, IBM

The man on the plane kept talking to himself. Not very loud, but loud enough that he could be heard. Then it got real interesting because not only was he talking to himself, he started answering.

When Terry was through talking to himself, he started a conversation with the person next to him. It turned out that Terry was a sales representative for IBM, and that he was on his way to make a presentation to a major client. When questioned about the previous conversation with himself, he did not call what he had been doing imagery, but what he was practicing had everything to do with imagery and peak sales performance.

All of the time Terry had been talking to himself, he had   actually been preparing for an upcoming presentation in Miami. To test out the objections and questions his upcoming presentation might stimulate, or leave unanswered, Terry said that he had pictured three of the toughest prospects he had ever met and had them all seated right in front of him. "These three were tough," he commented. "They interrupted, wanted proof of everything I said, went to sleep the second I was not interesting, and left no stone unturned." He said that if he could get through these three tough prospects then he could get through anything.

Thank you, "IBM." That is a great imagery technique for determining questions that can, and should, come up during the Conviction step of your sales process.

Your Turn

It is your turn to begin practicing the "IBM" technique.

- Go to your quiet place.
- Relax and begin breathing deeply.
- You are calm, quiet, relaxed and ready to begin answering questions.
- You are in front of three of your most demanding prospects. Look into each one of their faces one at a time. It has been a long day for all of them. They are tired, anxious to get home, and over budget. Their eyes are half-closed. You had better be interesting or they are going to fall asleep. You had better have something of real value or they are going to leave. And you had better be able to answer their questions or they are going to charge you for the time you have wasted.
- Remain calm, quiet, and relaxed.
- Start into the Conviction and Desire step of the sale and allow them to interrupt when they wish.
- Your mind is working freely.
- They continue asking you questions, and you are able to respond.
- When they ask a question you do not know the answer to, remain poised. Write it down and tell

them you will get back with them.
- Remember the formula is "mentally aware and physically poised."
- Continue answering their questions until you are through your entire presentation. Great practice session!

During your imagery practice session, you experienced the following:

Objections:

_____

_____

_____

_____

Questions:

_____

_____

_____

_____

Rejections:

_____

_____

_____

_____

Stalls:

_____

_____

_____

_____

Justifications:

_____

_____

_____

_____

From Your Imagery Practice

Several things will come from your working through the previous practice exercise. You can:

1. Discover the true value of having a firm presentation developed and integrated.

2. Discover questions about your offering that you do not have answers for. That is OK! Now is the time for that discovery, not with a prospect.

3. Practice transitions back into the Conviction and Desire step of the sale, and even back to the use of questioning techniques.

4. See, hear and feel yourself answering questions successfully, and nothing breeds success like success itself.

5. Develop confidence because you have been there.

Rid Yourself Of Irritations With Perceptual Flexibility

Two additional tools that support your selling on the "other side" and help in maintaining the physical poise and mental awareness you have been practicing throughout the book are:

1. PERCEPTUAL FLEXIBILITY
2. OBJECTIFICATION

The first technique of perceptual flexibility is developing your awareness that a situation can be viewed in more than one way. Every person's perspective is unique to them. Remember that you always have the option of how to interpret the results of a sales call. You are the one who looks at winning and losing. You decide whether to have fun or not have fun.

Is the glass half empty or half full? It is your decision, your construction of reality, your image, so you choose.

It Cannot Be Your Manager's Fault All The Time

One thing for you to decide right now is who's in control of your perceptions. Are you in control, or is "quota?" Are you in control or are "consequences?" How much control over your perceptions have you given up to your sales manager? Only one of you can drive the car, hit the golf ball, or take responsibility for moving the sale forward. Decide now, put the decision behind you, and travel on. Take control of your own actions and allow yourself to graduate to the next higher level of performance in sales.

When the sale does not progress according to your plan, you can perceive this either as a negative or as an opportunity to create an effective call out of demanding and challenging circumstances. The choice is yours.

Making this perceptual choice is an example of an NLP technique called "Reframing." It is the process of changing the "frame" or context in which we perceive our experiences, and by doing so, changing their meaning. Reframing is a very powerful tool, as it gives you the ability to replace destructive, negative images with positive images. The key is in finding constructive ways to satisfy the positive intention that lies at the heart of all negative behavior. Reframing can be helpful in a multitude of situations.

The professional golfer was playing in a tournament, stood up to her tee shot on the third hole and proceeded to hit a big hook right into the woods to her left—out of bounds for a two stroke penalty. She looked at her caddie and in all seriousness said, "What a great golf shot!" The lady playing in her foursome responded, "Are you nuts, or what? That was the worst hook I've seen in a long time and it cost you two stokes." Our player agreed with her and then said, "But that was also the exact image I had in my mind right before I hit the shot. Out of bounds and to the left."

She was right. She got exactly what she had imaged. Nice shot! Was the shot appropriate for the situation? NO. But how could it be called a BAD shot when her body did exactly what her mind was programed to do? It was a great shot, INAPPROPRIATE, but great. She had "reframed" the out-of-bounds shot as a positive experience.

She stayed poised, mentally put herself back into the golf game, and proceeded to put the next one right down the middle of the fairway. Another great shot, and this one was appropriate. She made the choice and demonstrated her perceptual flexibility.

In reality, an ineffective sales call can have a positive effect on your development. When the customer makes a decision in your favor, you can accept that your images were clear, controlled, appropriate, and that you maintained an effective level of physical poise and mental awareness. Congratulate yourself. If you did not get a decision in your favor, you can view it as an opportunity to improve your image clarity, along with your levels of poise, mental awareness and resourcefulness. It can be another learning opportunity for developing a positive experience base.

A sales trainer we worked with in Oregon told us about a student she had who was making the worst introduction into a sale you could possibly imagine. He was describing it in one of Linnaea's sales classes and said it was so bad that he wanted to throw up his hands, get out of his seat, and start all over. Well, that is exactly what he did. He got up, turned around and pointed back at the empty seat and said to the prospect, "Did you see that? That was the worst beginning to a sales call I have ever seen. Do you agree?" Then before the prospect could answer, he sat back down and said, "Now, let's get off on the right foot," and he started all over. That's perceptual flexibility! That young salesperson saw the event, and reframed it as an opportunity to improve instead of an opportunity to fail before the prospect. The fact that his opening remarks were not effective was irrelevant. It was what he chose to do about it that mattered.

Make a habit out of perceptual and behavioral flexibility and not only will you have more fun selling, but your success ratio will go up.

Take time out right now to practice PERCEPTUAL FLEXIBILITY.

- Go to your quiet place.
- Relax and become conscious of your breathing.
- You are calm, quiet, and relaxed.
- Allow yourself to relax.
- Go inside and recall a time to when you made a sales call that did not go as well as you would have liked. Re-create the entire sale in your mind. Hear the prospect's questions and see his face and gestures. Let it flow.
- Now process the question, "What positive outcome came out of that experience? What did I learn as a result of that call?"
- You are calm, quiet, and relaxed.

I learned from that call that:

_____

_____

_____

It was a valuable experience for me because:

_____

_____

_____

_____

Objectification

Objectification is a technique for REPLACING thoughts and emotions that are not to your advantage in sales. Rejection is an emotion with which most of us in sales are all too familiar. Physically, rejection can translate into stress and tension. Some salespeople find that the effects of disappointment and stress travel and take up residence in their necks, lower backs, and all over their bodies. When you have mastered the objectification technique, you can take those vague feelings of stress, turn them into OBJECTS you can dispose of, and then replace those objects with something you like and can enjoy.

Here are those four steps in objectification:

1. IDENTIFY THE EMOTION YOU WANT TO GET RID OF AND LOCATE IT IN YOUR BODY. Is it in your stomach? Neck? Back? Where is it? You have to pin it down specifically.

2. USE ALL OF YOUR SENSES TO TURN THAT EMOTION INTO A CONCRETE OBJECT. Give that emotion size, shape, color, texture, temperature, smell, and determine whether or not it makes any noises. Is it solid like a rock, or burning like a fire?

3. DISPOSE OF THE OBJECT. Mentally image it as you launch it into outer space, put it into a big hole and cover it up, or put it down your garbage disposal. Just get rid of it!

4. REPLACE THE OBJECT WITH SOMETHING YOU

LIKE. This is key. Replace that object with something you perceive will contribute to your being physically poised and mentally aware. Fill in all of the details about this new object and you will find commitment in that level of detail. Did you fill the space with ice cream, with a cool ocean breeze, or with the warmth of the sun? Fill it all up.

One example of implementing this technique came from a sales manager in an investment services firm in Portland, Oregon. His firm would go to great lengths working up a proposal for clients, often to the tune of $3,OOO for each presentation. If their proposals were rejected in favor of another firm, Mike would get so upset that it not only ruined that particular day but the next day as well, and even hurt his golf game. Well, Mike knew that when rejection hurt his golf game, it was time to take action.

Most of the discomfort from Mike's lost sale was located in the middle of his stomach. He actually felt it right in the middle. Mike said that it was as if someone had gotten in there and tied his stomach into knots. It was a very definite feeling of pain and anger. Using objectification, Mike turned that emotion into a little red man, the devil himself, who was down there making spaghetti out of his insides. Mike could feel the heat coming off the devil, he could smell the fire burning where the devil was working, and he could see the spaghetti getting all knotted up. The colors were very vivid and he could feel the pain every time the devil forced his pitchfork into the spaghetti. To get rid of all this mess he took the devil, wrapped him in the spaghetti, pulled him out, and threw him down the garbage disposal. He could see himself throwing the devil into the disposal, turning on the switch, and listening to the sweet sound of his being ground up and washed out to sea in the flood of water. Then he replaced that big hole with a double scoop of triple chocolate ice cream. Cool, smooth, chocolate ice cream that he could taste, smell, feel, and see. Hear the sound of the ice cream going into that great big hole!

The purpose of both objectification and perceptual flexibility is to provide you with specific techniques to rid yourself of irritations and tensions that build and prevent you from devoting 100% of your positive and productive energy to each prospect and to yourself. These are just two more of the techniques that help you get to, and remain at, peak levels of sales performance.

When Not To Answer Questions

Five times NOT to answer questions from prospects:

1. When you do not know the answer. Do not fake it. Tell prospects that you do not know, and then go find the answer and report back to them.

2. When a specialist in your organization needs to be consulted for a more accurate response.

3. When you cannot commit your organization to the prospect's request.

4. When the prospect phrases an idea in the form of a statement rather than a question. These veiled statements usually end with the words, "Don't you agree?"

5. When you know that the prospect is fully capable of answering their own question.

A Reminder—Salespeople Create 80% Of All Objections

Do not allow yourself to fall in with the 80% of all salespeople who create objections during the buying process because of their own incomplete prospect qualification, preparation, ineffective questioning techniques, and unfounded presentations.

*You Are In The Top 20% Of
All Salespeople!*

10

Even The Worst Drunk In
All Of Texas Serves as
a Great Bad Example

Action Step Of The Sale

SALES CYCLE   PROSPECT
                              BUYING CYCLE

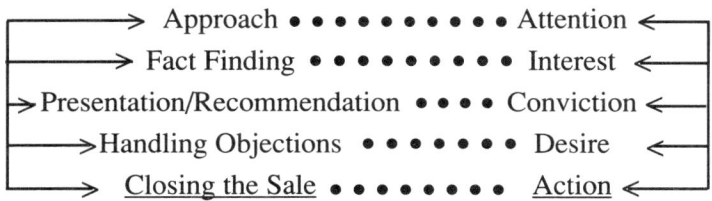

"You don't always have to present good examples for people to learn," said E.K. "Shoot, even the worst, fallen down, stone blind drunk in all of Texas isn't all bad. Man, he serves as a great BAD EXAMPLE."

E.K. was a great sales trainer. He had probably learned more about human nature and how to get along with more kinds of people than any salesperson or trainer around. He taught a lot of people how to sell, even with some of the "bad examples" he employed.

A sales manager that I worked for early in my sales career taught me a great deal that I remain thankful for even today. Larry was a man that our sale group both looked up to and respected. However, as good a sales manager and salesperson as Larry was, one sales call we made provides an effective "bad example" for getting a decision in your favor during a sales call.

Larry and I were out on the road making sales calls together. It was getting late in the afternoon, our time was limited, we had a hundred miles left to drive when the day was over, and we were particularly anxious to "close" a sale with the particular client we were about to call on. The customer was a long way from our office. A return trip would take an additional sales day, and we wanted to get the decision right then and there.

Years have dulled the details of the exact conversation with the customer, but it remains clear that Larry and I did everything we could to "close" that sale. Well, we got the sale closed, the contract signed, and were on our long drive back home. When we got into the office the next morning, you already know the message that was waiting for us. It was from the customer we had "closed" the afternoon before and he had decided NOT to purchase our product.

We had forced the door to the sale closed, the prospect reacted, knocked the door back open, and knocked the sale back over on us. We had moved away from the basic premise of focusing on the prospect, had placed the entire focus on our needs and wants, and had gotten exactly what we deserved. The problem in this situation was not in closing the sale. We knew the "secrets" to closing; we just forgot about the secret of getting a lasting decision in our favor. THERE IS A DIFFERENCE!

Getting A Decision In Your Favor

The purpose of this step in the sales process is to have the prospect make a commitment to the predetermined action that you have been building up to during the entire sales process. Always remember that:

**IN MAKING A PURCHASE DECISION,
THE FEAR OF LOSS IS GREATER THAN
THE ANTICIPATION OF GAIN**

The larger the sale, the more important this statement becomes in the buying process.

Exercise

- Go to your quiet place.
- Relax. Pay attention to your breathing.
- You are calm, quiet, and relaxed.
- Now, using the sensory images, feelings, or sounds that work best for you, process the images associated with these words: "Getting a decision in my favor happens, it is not something I do."
- Invest several minutes of these images: "Success happens, it is not something I do."

My images associated with "getting a decision in my favor" were:

_____

_____

_____

_____

Because of a mistaken concept of closing, far too often we have observed sales calls turning into a form of competition between the salesperson and the prospect. The salesperson mistakenly begins to view "closing" the sale as a victory, as winning, as the final objective. With that thought in mind, here is another exercise for your perceptual flexibility.

- Remain in your quiet place.
- Relax. Pay attention to your breathing.
- You are calm, quiet, and relaxed.
- Now process the images, words, sounds and inner feelings associated with the word "winning."
- Ask yourself, "What is winning, really? Do I have to be #1 at something to have won?"
- Now ask yourself, "How do I really win with prospects?"
  "How do I really win with my company?"
  "How do I really win with myself?"
  "How do I really win with the relationships in my life?"
- Only you have the images for these questions.

For me, winning in sales is:

_____

_____

_____

_____

For the customer, winning is:

_____

_____

_____

_____

For my company, winning is:

_____

_____

Constantly Changing Variables

Let's add another dimension to getting a decision in your favor.

Add 1 and 1 and the result is 2.

Add 1 and 1 again, and this time the result is O.

Now add 1 and 1, only this time please consider that the result can be 3.

Getting a buying decision in your favor is much the same as adding 1 and 1 in the three examples given above. In these examples what do the numbers 2, O, and 3 all have in common?

You got it. They were all THE RESULT. In sales you have had, or will have, those days when you did everything right, the prospect was right and you were in rapport with him, the situation was right, and you got a decision in your favor. On the next sales call everything seemed to go the same way, except the decision went against you. Then on the last sales call of the day nothing seemed to go right, yet the prospect decided to take twice the amount you had anticipated. It seemed to you that the elements remained pretty much the same, but the RESULTS varied.

The sales lesson is to focus on the elements that you have the most control over, which include elements within the process, and not on the elements that you have less control over, which is the result. Focusing on results means that you have become detached or disassociated. It is NOT selling in the here-and-now.

Change Is Constant

Dr. Gary Wiren (noted author and golf professional) defines the game of golf as "a game of constantly changing variables." The more Dr. Wiren talks about the game of golf, the clearer it becomes that he is not only talking about golf but about sales as well. You can enhance your performance and help more people by defining sales as a game/profession of constantly changing variables.

Consider the FACT that you are in a constant stage of minor change. In fact, in the three seconds that it just took for you to read that last sentence, 15 million cells in your body have changed. That is right. Your body produces 15 million new cells, the new you, each second. You change and your prospects change as well. Ever had one of your long-standing clients change right before your very eyes? If not, you will. Business situations differ, prices and values fluctuate, prospect needs and wants go up and down, and even your products are altered. Sales really is a game/profession of CONSTANTLY CHANGING VARIABLES.

On the positive side, change is what keeps sales a fun, creative process for you. When positive change ceases to be your perception of reality, check your "perceptual flexibility." It may need an adjustment.

How Do I Get A Decision In My Favor?

Let's take a lesson on getting a sales decision in your favor from a successful baseball pitcher. When you watch the pitching arm of a successful baseball pitcher, you will learn a very valuable lesson about getting a sales decision in your favor. When a pitcher's fastball is working, really working, the pitcher's arm goes THROUGH a very precise series of movements. The emphasis on this sentence, and the pitching sequence, is that his arm processes through an effective sequence. There is no way in the world that pitcher can SET his arm into that position in a vacuum. His arm does not get into the correct position as an independent act—if he ever attempted to get his arm into that correct position by focusing just on that one movement, the pitch just would not happen.The pitcher's arm GETS TO the correct position only as it moves through an effective sequence or rotation. The same principle applies to your selling. When you attempt to get a decision in your favor by focusing on just the Action step of the sales process, that step typically will not happen. The PROCESS is important, not the individual steps.

You are reading this book with the expectation of learning more about how to get a decision in your favor. With this expectation in mind, what you will do is take a technique from this step of the sales process, remove it from the total process, work to habituate it, and then reinstall it into the total process.

To facilitate the learning process, let's turn to the oldest newspaper questioning technique in existence—Who? Why? What? When? Where? and, How?

Who?

WHO IS THE DECISION-MAKER?

This sounds like an easy question, but is it? You know that between the day you started selling and now, you have already missed several attempts to get a decision in your favor because you were NOT talking with the actual decision-maker. And this does not always involve calling at the top of an organization. So, an important step is to learn WHO in a family or firm makes the final decision where your products are concerned. Where is the best place to find this out? Right again—in the preparation step of the sale, which is before your sales call.

Why?

WHY ARE YOU SELLING?

This question takes you right back to your basic attitude for sales, your INtent in sales. Why are you working to get a decision in your favor? ANSWER: YOU ARE NOT! You are out there working to get a decision that mutually benefits both you and the prospect. When your selling is not a win-win situation for you, your company, and the prospect, you are not working to establish long-term customer relationships and you are after short-term sales results for yourself. When it IS a win-win situation for both parties, you are selling from a basis of well-formed goals and outcomes for your prospect and yourself.

Ask yourself a question (talking to yourself is great practice for sales). "Is that last statement always true? Does there always have to be a win-win situation?"

Ask yourself this question:

QUESTION: When you play a game, any game, how do you know when you have won?

ANSWER: One definition of winning is that you feel better after the game than before! And you feel good about having participated. THINK ABOUT IT. You do not have to agree or disagree, but please think about this possible definition for winning.

How should you feel when you have "won" at sales?

How should your prospects feel when they have "won" at buying?

How should your company feel about the transaction?

Right again. All parties concerned should feel better

than when the process started. That is a win-win result.

When?

WHEN DO YOU GET THE DECISION?
The "when" element of the formula has two major components. First, ask for a decision only when the prospect is aware of VALUE. In a win-win situation, value is exchanged for value. Prospects will not make valid decisions until they are aware of the value they are giving in relation to the value they are receiving. Thinking of value more in terms of a trade than a sale may help your sales performance. Focus on your prospect trading value for value.

The next element of "when" comes directly from the prospect.

Prospects have a unique way of communicating to you when they have made their decisions. The discussion is about . . .

YOUR house
YOUR warranty
YOUR terms

Keep your ears open for the next thing you know, prospects can switch on you and begin talking about . . .

THEIR house
THEIR warranty
THEIR terms

Listen for the prospect's vocabulary to switch to POSSESSIVE TERMS AND WORDS (our, my, mine) and you can pick up an indicator as to when they have made a decision. Often times you are actually aware of a prospect's decision to act BEFORE they are. When this occurs, all you have to do is let the prospect know about the decision they have already made.

How?

HOW DO YOU GET A DECISION IN YOUR FAVOR?
In many sales instances, "negotiation" represents the essence of the decision making process, or of getting a decision in your favor. There is no close, no secret set of words to change prospects into customers, only the discussing, bargaining, and decision making process of two business people working out the mutually acceptable terms of a business relationship. Negotiation is one key to action and to getting a decision in your favor.

Do not forget to ask for a decision in your favor. When all of your senses tell you the decision has already been made in your favor, ask for it! So many salespeople circle the airport for so long that they forget their original objective was to land the plane. When you feel or observe that the decision has been made, ask the prospect!

QUESTION: Why don't more salespeople just come right out and ask for the decision when they already sense that the prospect has made it?

ANSWER: There is more than one answer to this question, but more often than not you have been trained out of the habit of asking for what you want or think you deserve. Many of you have become too "technique" oriented. What you have is "sales paralysis by analysis."

By now you have the image. Too many salespeople have been trained out of the habit of asking for that which they believe to be rightly earned. They have been trained into using techniques to work around a situation, not go straight to the solution. When paralysis by analysis happens to you, how do you change it? Like any other ineffective habit, do not give up the old habit. You concentrate on forming a new and more effective habit. When you are deserving, have proven the value of your product, and sense the decision has already been made, start asking the prospect for their business.

Fear Of Rejection

There are also those salespeople who seldom ask for a decision because when they do, they run the risk of being turned down. To them, not getting a decision in their favor is a rejection of them, the individual. These salespeople think in terms of their being turned down, their being wrong, their being shot in the back, disgraced, and run into the ground. When these are the images you associate with sales and rejection, they will drive you right out of the business.

Ask yourself another question. What is the difference between a prospect saying "no" to your business offer and saying "no" to you as an individual?

There is a major difference. Nine times out of ten, prospects are rejecting the OFFER, not the individual. How about that other one time? Nobody is perfect and neither are you. We all have individual profiles and tendencies, and we all work with prospects on a different basis. This is not to say that we do not have room for improvement. What we are saying is to take rejection as input, feedback, learn from it, and have the flexibility to adjust to it accordingly and when appropriate.

When You Are Good, All You Need Is An Opportunity To Prove It

Here is something that may help put your current techniques into a better perspective for peak performance in sales. Some of the most effective sales calls occur when you allow the prospect to do the bulk of the work, including the talking.

Ever have a prospect make the sales presentation for you? Refine and habituate the following approach and your prospects will make a lot more decisions in your favor.

A real sales pro from the hospitality industry made a call on a prospect that had never done business with either him or his conference center. Frank had done a very good job of getting into casual conversation with the meeting planner of this particular firm and had confirmed the information he gathered during preparation. Then he switched gears and allowed the prospect to take off in high gear.

Frank asked the prospect for three or four things he really liked about the conference center where they were currently holding the bulk of their meetings and conventions. The prospect gave him three positive features of their current vendor and threw in another for good measure. Frank then asked for the one thing the prospect might change about the conference center if he could. There was not one thing the prospect could come up with. Not one!

Something very interesting happened then. Frank mentally moved over to the prospect's side of the desk and let him know that he was pleased he had found a home for his meetings. At that point, Frank sounded more like a business associate than a salesperson. He was actually congratulating the other man on his decision and work with the other conference center.

Frank thought for a moment, looked up into space for another moment, then turned his head back to face the prospect and asked him dead center, "Do you carry car insurance?" The prospect's response was an obvious "yes." Frank paused again, then asked, "And how about life insurance? Do you carry any?" Again, a "yes" response from the prospect.

His final question to the prospect was, "Then how about meeting insurance? What happens when you have an emergency meeting, need extra space, and they have a problem at the hotel you are using. What do you do then?"

Frank was very smart. He didn't pause for a second but kept right on going. "All I want," he said, "is the chance to let you know that we can perform when you need us. We can be your meeting back-up, your insurance. But, BEFORE you trust us, you had better try us out. When is the first meeting you can hold with us and check us out?"

Frank not only got their next meeting, but he got two more meetings just like it from other prospects that same day. The moral of Frank's story is that you and your offering are good, really good, so all you need or want from prospects is the OPPORTUNITY TO PROVE YOUR VALUE.

Far too often salespeople go after a commitment that prospects are just not prepared, or willing, to make. This is when salespeople attempt to build units of value on unfirm foundations. Salespeople call on a prospect for the first time, the prospect does not even know them, and that same salesperson is actually asking the prospect to immediately feel rapport with him and trust him.

Give yourself a break. Do you realize that you have even been allowing yourself to get upset when brand new prospects do not make a major decision in your favor? They do not even know you, why should they trust you with their business? What kind of sense, let alone dollars, does that make? Is that an open- or closed-ended question? Does it really make any real difference?

A "Closing" Statement About Sales Techniques

When we first presented the DiSC "Prospect Classification" system in a training workshop in St. Louis, Missouri, one of the participants made a very astute observation. Amanda commented that the classification system had more to do with getting decisions in her favor than with any other step in the sales process.

Amanda observed that in getting a decision in her favor it was not always which technique she used, but rather HOW she used the technique or approach. Rather than have five techniques to help prospects take action, what she really needed was three techniques that she could use effectively with the four different groups of prospects in the DiSC model. We think Amanda was basically correct.

Look at a specific sales technique, the "minor-decision" method of helping a prospect take action, and see if you agree with Amanda.

"Minor-Decision" Method

With this method, you ask prospects a question where they need to make a decision; a minor decision, not a major one. When you ask the prospect, "Will you purchase or not purchase," that is a major decision. It takes prospects time to make major decisions, so ask for minor decisions and make it easier for them to become customers.

This technique is effective not because it is a trick, but because this is the way prospects process information. It is difficult for many prospects to change. And it is difficult for prospects to make major decisions, especially when we have high "C" and "S" buying profiles.

This technique includes always asking for a decision between "something" and "something," not between "something" and "nothing." A buy/not buy, decision is between "something" (buy) and "nothing" (not buy).

"Do you want the safety deposit box in your name, or do you want it listed jointly with your son?" This question offers the prospect a choice between "something" (they sign and own) and "something" (joint signature and ownership). Let's quickly review your DiSC model and then look at it in reference to the "Minor-Decision" sales technique just presented.

Behavior Pattern	Tendencies Toward Making Decisions & Taking Action
"D" Dominance	*Cause action
	*Risk-taking
	*Quick decisions
	*Immediate results
"I" Influencing	*Freedom from detail
	*Emotional
	*Verbal
	*Optimistic
"S" Steadiness	*Patient
	*Security oriented
	*Slow to change
	*Calculated
	*Low risk-taking
"C" Compliance	*Critical thinking
	*Check for accuracy
	*No sudden changes
	*Logical
	*Analysis of data

Source: Performax Systems International, Inc.

"D"/Dominance Prospects

Once dominant prospects perceive value, you can typically get some quick results from using the "Minor-Decision" technique.

Prospects with high "D" tendencies tend to take action based on fewer facts than other groups, and they seem to enjoy making decisions more than the other groups.

PLEASE NOTE: We are not looking for a "quick sale" with any of our four prospect groups, and are only talking about the length of time in this one step of the sale and helping prospects make decisions once they perceive the value.

STATEMENTS ATTRACTIVE TO THIS GROUP:

"This is a totally new approach; there really is nothing else like it on the market today."

"Take it and give it a try."

Your statement:

_____

_____

_____

_____

"I"/Influencing Prospects

This group of prospects tends to make decisions from an emotional perspective rather than from pure logic. They may be more "kinesthetic" people—more in touch with their physical and emotional feelings. You can make the "Minor-Decision" technique very helpful to them. The question you present in the technique actually serves to keep these prospects on track, focused on the task at hand, and supports their decision-making process.

STATEMENTS ATTRACTIVE TO THIS GROUP:

"This is a summary that will help you see the practicality of the product."

"A few of the people in the community using this service that you might know are . . ."

Your statement:

_____

_____

_____

_____

"S"/Steadiness Prospects

Prospects high in this tendency tend to change very slowly unless given REASONS for change. You do not need to keep this group focused, as with high "I" prospects. High "S" prospects are typically very good listeners and process information in an orderly fashion. They tend to reach their own decisions at the appropriate step in the process.

High "S" prospects are typically well organized and patient. Using the technique can only help them reach a decision once they are already at that point in their more logical decision making process.

STATEMENTS ATTRACTIVE TO THIS GROUP:

"Let's actually walk you through how we make a commercial loan. That will give you an opportunity to see what it's really going to take for us to qualify you."

"By having moved up to this next level of performance, you are really achieving a form of insurance for yourself and your family. There is just more security at this level."

Your statement:

_____

_____

_____

_____

"C"/Compliance Prospects

Individuals with this behavioral trait tend to emphasize the importance of making decisions based on factual data. The process of decision-making and problem solving may not be as important to them as the number of facts in favor of making the "perfect" decision.

Individuals with high "C" tendencies can be uncomfortable with assertive salespeople and may have difficulty making a decision. Use your "Minor-Decision" technique to help these prospects come to logical conclusions.

STATEMENTS ATTRACTIVE TO THIS GROUP:

"A product such as this must have standards which will allow you to carefully evaluate its quality over time. This product will stand up to both your expectations and evaluations."

"You are probably in the best position to look at all of the facts, interpret them yourself, and come to a conclusion."

Your statement:

_____

_____

_____

_____

What do you think? Your perspective is the important one!

Be Good To Yourself In Learning And Habituating These New Techniques

11

Vote Early And
Vote Often

Implementation

It has been said that Mayor Daley's voting instructions
in Chicago were, "Vote early and vote often." For your
mental practice and habituation of the ideas and techniques presented in this book, our instructions are much the
same. "Practice early, and practice often." Add to that,
"practice regularly." Remember that mental practice and
visualization are the same as being there!

At some point in almost every sales seminar, someone
turns the discussion to the subject of the "natural" salesperson. The same thing happens in sports workshops and
participants still want to know about the "natural" athlete.

Would you want to be operated on by a "natural" doctor? If Boston General Hospital ever found a natural doctor, graduated her at the top of her class with no training,
and you were on her operating table, what would you think
of that natural doctor?

Or how about a "natural" lawyer? Harvard Law School
found that "natural" lawyer! They have already graduated
him at the top of his class without having put him through

any training. Now, here is the situation. You are on trial for your life. Do you want that "natural" lawyer as your attorney?

The answers to both questions should be a resounding "No!" Then why do people want to talk about a "natural" salesperson? True, we all have the POTENTIAL for achieving greatness in the field of sales. But by design, training, development, and practice, that potential must be refined and developed on an individual basis.

In a conversation with another sales trainer, Jerry commented that he reads where successful salespeople die, but he never reads about successful salespeople being born. Therefore he concluded that sometime between birth and death, those salespeople must have been trained.

Skills cannot be given away or received, they must be earned and developed. To develop the ideas and concepts presented in this book into skills, regular, frequent, and continued practice must be applied in liberal doses.

Become Your Own Support System

One of the more notable features of this book is the absence of instructions telling you the exact ways to approach a prospect, probing techniques to determine information you want, fifteen ways to make a presentation, six ways to handle objections, and fifty ways to close a sale. The book does offer limited input as to which techniques to use, when to use them, how your prospect might react to them, and the variety of applications of the same techniques.

What we DO want you to focus on, integrate, and apply are:

1. YOUR habituation of effective sales skills
2. Total conceptualization of YOUR attitudes and behavior toward people

3. YOUR devotion to purpose
4. YOUR perfect practice
5. YOUR imagination and excellent sensory acuity skills
6. YOU are your own best support system

This focus is necessary for you to become proficient in helping others through sales and for your own enjoyment through the journey. To help and support others, you must first learn to help and support yourself.

Secrets Every Peak Performer Knows

Obtaining top achievement in sales means making choices. When you say YES to a sales goal or related objective, you are saying NO to some other area of your work or private life. Success does have its price, and in our training programs we do not bother placing any faith in the popular commercial that says, "You can have it all." Success means choices, and at times very difficult choices. Successful salespeople just happen to think the choices are worth making.

On "secret," if there is such a thing, it may be that successful salespeople do not dwell on the things they must give up. They focus positively on what they, and their prospects, can earn.

Is Practice Necessary?

Yes, practice is necessary, but only perfect practice makes perfect and it needs to be practice that you ENJOY doing. Do not always focus on "paying the price" or on the amount of time you invest in sales practice. We do not always enjoy paying the price. Customers want to enjoy the rewards, and so should you. Focus on both you and your customer's ENJOYING THE REWARDS of your sales efforts and training! Focus on seeing your prospect's problems solved, on hearing their enthusiastic comments, and feeling their friendly handshake.

Sales is a career to be enjoyed. Be creative. Find out what selling and performing with creativity and enjoyment really are like. Sarah, a swimmer on a Florida team we worked with, was talking about practicing every morning, and then again every afternoon, for twelve months a year. "Do you love to swim that much?" we asked.

"I have been loving it for five years now."

"Is it fun for you?" we asked.

"No!" she responded. "It's rewarding."

Sarah had learned from her swimming career what many salespeople experience; the real "love" and "reward" that develops from the steps of:

Self-Discipline
Self-Control
Self-Confidence
Self-Realization

Take In All Of The Information You Can Process

Take in all the information you can from books, magazines, good salespeople, and every resource available to you. Weigh this information in light of your fundamentals and the concept of your own modeling and ideas. You will quickly disregard eighty percent of incoming advice and information as a quick fix or as being inaccurate. You will watch the skills of effective salespeople and understand WHY and HOW they perform as well as they do. You will observe successful athletes and realize the same thing.

Interpret these observations, synthesize and reform the image to fit the individual person you are and your unique perspective.

It is not only okay to be on your own during much of this process, but perhaps essential for your success. Participate in your own development with the notion of improvement, not as a one-time goal, but as an ongoing process that ultimately helps you, your prospect, and your organization.

The Value Of Experience

We have said it before, but it may be worth repeating, that there are some sales skills that can be learned but cannot be taught.

In sports, guiding someone through the learning process of how to take a putter and strike a golf ball with the exact energy required to roll it a set distance is a classic example of self-learning. There are some very strange and equally useless pieces of advice out there to tell golfers how to hit a putt. In truth, EXPERIENCE is the teacher for determining the proper energy required to hit a ball a predetermined distance. Your perception of the hole and the surrounding conditions provoke the calculation. Sales is a very similar type of learning experience. Your calculations for helping a prospect become an image that is then transferred to action through kinesthetic sensory processes. The evaluation of the outcome forms another image of how you worked with that individual prospect. Repeating this experience, and the image-making process, is how your unique system learns the proper response to the givens provided by the prospect and the conditions at hand.

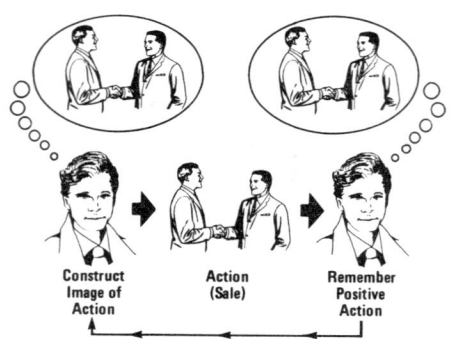

Construct   Action   Remember
Image of   (Sale)   Positive
Action   Action

THIS IS THE CREATIVE PROCESS IN SALES AT ITS
BEST. This creativity can be practiced on the walls of your
mind. Creativity is the part of sales to be relished, lived in,
and allowed to develop.

A Major Barrier To Implementation

The sales manager has a quota in mind for you to reach.
The basketball coach has a certain number of points she
expects you to score for the season. The teacher has a
predetermined passing grade for you to make. Everyone
has their expectations of you and of your results.
As a sales manager, as a professional sales trainer, and as a
professional sports trainer, I certainly understand the
importance of results. But I believe that more harm continues to be done by individuals setting outcome goals
rather than performance goals than any other factor. It is
important for your success in sales to remember that you
do not implement results. You cannot do a goal. You
implement that which you have the most control over. You
do activities. Therefore, as you are learning and beginning
to implement the techniques and ideas from this resource,
remember to focus on performance improvement AC-

TIVITIES over time.

Before working through your sales goals, let's look at basketball for an example of implementation.

INAPPROPRIATE SPORTS GOAL FOR #44:

Winning the basketball game.

Why is "winning" an inappropriate goal?

What elements of the basketball game does player #44 NOT have control over?

- The other team.
- The officials.
- The coach.
- What if #44 is ill?
- What if #44 does not get to play?
- And the list can go on and on.

The very goals that #44 is creating can be setting #44 up for failure. The key is to establish goals and objectives in areas where #44 has a higher degree of control.

MORE APPROPRIATE GOAL FOR #44:

From prior practice and game performance, #44 sets a goal to: In the next game, make 64% of the shots taken within the appropriate shooting zone, when a defender is two feet or further away, and when a pass into the court is not more appropriate. Now, while you can improve on both the writing and appropriateness of this sports goal, it is a least a start towards a goal that #44 CAN PERFORM AND MEASURE.

INAPPROPRIATE SALES GOAL:

To make $200,000 in sales this year.

Why is this an inappropriate goal for you?

What elements of the process do you NOT have control over?

- The competition.

- The legal environment.
- Your own company.
- Your manager.
- Pricing.
- Your product offering.
- What if you are injured on the job?
- And the list could go on and on.

MORE APPROPRIATE SALES GOAL:

From prior practice and sales performance, you set a goal to: Learn to generate twenty new qualified prospects a week from your existing customer base by using a proven referral technique. Again, while you could improve on both the writing and appropriateness of this goal, it is at least a start towards a goal that you CAN PERFORM AND MEASURE.

Please recall our goal setting suggestion from *The One Minute Golfer*.

a. Set immediate goals.

b. Set short-term goals.

c. Set long-term goals.

d. AND you cannot do a goal, you accomplish objectives that take you towards your goal.

Now for your own sales year!

The following is a goal that you have set, or that has been set for you, that you consider as inappropriate to implement:

_____

_____

_____

_____

A more appropriate goal would be to:

(Note: this will probably be only one element of the major outcome goal that was written above.)

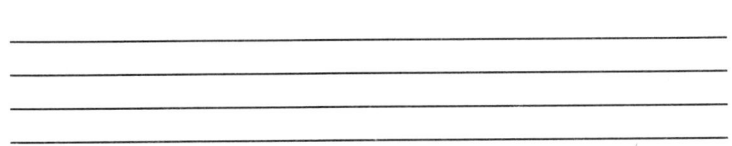

It will take additional time and space for you to process through your goals and recreate them in the form of process goals. This time is an investment in your sales career, not an expense.

Read Their Book

Ken Blanchard's *The One Minute Manager* is suggested reading, but until you get the chance to read or review the book, here is page 34 on One Minute Goal Setting . . .

1. Agree on your goals. (Determine well-formed goals.)

2. See what acceptable behavior looks like. (Develop your skills in observing others.)

3. Write out each of your goals on a single sheet of paper using less than 250 words.

4. Read and re-read each goal, which requires only a minute or so each time you do it.

5. Take a minute every once in a while out of your day to look at your performance.

6. See whether or not your behavior matches (is congruent with) your goals.

Last On The List, But Perhaps First In Importance

Be sure to have FUN and stay mentally flexible throughout your sales journey to peak performance because you never do get "there." You are it, today is it, right now is it, and you will discover that there is no other place to get but the place you make for yourself and others. Do not wait to enjoy the result, learn to enjoy the process.

Your Beginning, Not The End

Bibliography & Resource Guide

GENERAL SALES

Alessandra, Dr. Anthony; Wexler, Phil; and Barrara, Rick, *Non-Manipulative Selling*, 2nd Edition, 1987, Prentice Hall Press.

Alessandra, Dr. Anthony and Cathcart, Jim, *The Business Of Selling: How To Be Your Own Sales Manager*, 1984, Reston Publishing Company.

Gayle, Willie, *Power Selling*, 1959, Prentice-Hall.

Hanan, Mack; Cribbin, James; and Heiser, Herman, *Consultative Selling*, 1973, AMACOM, a division of American Management Association.

Hanan, Mack; Cribbin, James; and Berrian, Howard, *Sales Negotiation Strategies*, 1977, AMACOM, a division of American Management Association.

Hanan, Mack; Cribbin, James; and Donis, Jack, *Systems Selling Strategies: How To Justify Premium Prices For Commodity Products*, 1978, AMACOM, a division of American Management Association.

Hopkins, Tom, *How To Master The Art Of Selling*, 2nd Edition, 1982, The Champion Press.

Mandino, Og, *The Greatest Salesman In The World*, 1968, Bantam Books.

Richardson, Linda, *Bankers In The Selling Role: A Consultative Guide To Cross-Selling Financial Services*, 1981,

John Wiley & Sons, Inc.

Savage, John, *High Touch Selling: How To Make A Great Life While Making A Great Living*, 1986, Farnsworth Publishing.

Ziglar, Zig, *See You At The Top*, 1975, Pelican.

SALES PSYCHOLOGY

Buzzotta, V.R.; Lefton, R.E.; and Sherberg, Manuel, *Effective Selling Through Psychology*, 1982, Ballinger Publishing Company, a division of Harper & Row, Publishers, Inc.

Lewis, Byron A. and Pucelik, Frank R., *Magic Demystified: An Introduction To Neuro-linguistic Programming*, 1982, Metamorphous Press.

Ostrander, Sheila, and Schroeder, Lynn, *Super-Learning*, 1979, Dell Publishing Co., Inc.

Whitney, Robert A.; Hubin, Thomas; and Murphy, John D., *The New Psychology Of Persuasion And Motivation In Selling*, 1965, Prentice-Hall, Inc.

GENERAL SALES/MARKETING/OTHER

Blanchard, Dr. Kenneth, and Johnson, Dr. Spencer, *The One Minute Manager*, 1982, William Morrow and Company, Inc.

Cooper, Ken, *Nonverbal Communication For Business Success*, 1979, AMACOM, a division of American Management Associations.

Engle, James F.; Kollat, David T.; and Blackwell, Roger D., *Consumer Behavior*, 3rd Edition, 1978, The Dryden Press.

Kotler, Philip, *Principles Of Marketing*, 3rd Edition, 1986, Prentice-Hall.

McCormack, Mark H., *What They Don't Teach You At Harvard Business School*, 1984, Bantam.

Molloy, John T., *Dress For Success*, 1975, Warner Books.
Russell, Bill and Branch, Taylor, *Second Wind: The Memoirs Of An Opinionated Man*, 1979, Random House.
Winston, Stephanie, *The Organized Executive: New Ways to Manage Time, Paper, and People*, 1983, W. W. Norton and Company.
Zikmund, William, and D'Amico, Michael, *Marketing*, 2nd Edition, 1986, John Wiley & Sons.

INTER-PERSONAL SKILLS
Bolton, Robert, *People Skills: How To Assert Yourself, Listen To Others, And Resolve Conflicts*, 1979, Prentice-Hall, Inc.
Gordon, Thomas, *Leader Effectiveness Training: L.E.T.*, 1977, Bantam Books.
Leider, Richard J. and Harding, James S., *Taking Charge*, 1985, Leider/Harding Enterprises, Inc.

STRESS MANAGEMENT/RELAXATION/IMAGERY
Benson, Herbert with Klipper, Miriam Z., *The Relaxation Response*, 1975, Avon Books.
Gawain, Shakti, *Creative Visualization*, 1982, Bantam Books.
Selye, Hans, *Stress Without Distress*, 1974, Signet Books, New American Library.

GENERAL HEALTH/WELLNESS
Note: Your general health and wellness is important to your overall success in sales and living.
Cooper, Kenneth, *The Aerobics Program For Total Well-being: Exercise, Diet, And Emotional Balance*, 1982, Bantam Books.
Garfield, Charles, *Peak Performers: The New Heroes of*

American Business, 1986, Garfield Enterprises Inc.

Garfield, Charles, *Peak Performance: Mental Training Techniques Of The World's Greatest Athletes,* 1984, Warner Books, Inc.

Haas, Robert, *Eat To Succeed: The Haas Maximum Performance Program,* 1986, Rawson Associates.

Loehr, James E., *Mental Toughness Training For Sports: Achieving Athletic Excellence,* 1982, The Stephen Greene Press.

MAGAZINE ARTICLES

Blanchard, Dr. Kenneth, and Toski, Bob, *The One Minute Golfer,* June 1985, *Golf Digest.*

A special thanks to the kind people at Performax Systems International, Inc. for allowing me the liberal use of ideas, materials, and concepts from their many publications. The primary materials used were:

Personal Profile System, Performax Systems International, Inc., 1979.
The Value Analysis Profile, 1985.

For more information on the these profiles, and related information, please contact Jim Robertson at Metamorphous Press, P.O. Box 10616, Portland, OR 97210-0616.

AUDIO TAPES

How To Master The Art Of Selling Anything by Tom Hopkins, 1980, Champions Unlimited, P.O. Box 1969, 7531 East 2nd Street, Scottsdale, Arizona, 85252.

Neuropsychology Of Achievement, 1985, Sybervision Systems, Inc., Fountain Square, 6066 Civic Terrace Ave., Neward, CA 94560.

Non-Manipulative Selling by Alessandra, Anthony J., and Wexler, Phillip S., Alessandra and Associates, P.O. Box 2767, La Jolla, CA 92038.

Psychology Of Winning by Denis E. Waitley, Nightingale-Conant Corporation, The Human Resources Company, Chicago, IL., 60641.

Relaxation Tapes. For additional information on training tapes and materials, write to James E. Robertson at Metamorphous Press, P.O. Box 10616, Portland, OR, 97210-0616

Self-Discipline, 1986, Sybervision Systems. See address on previous page.

James E. Robertson

Author—Teacher—Trainer
Consultant—Saleperson

In the world of sales, Jim has been there. Whether you are talking about selling internationally, selling large computer system, retail sales, or marketing services, Jim has been there.

Scholastics need to be tempered with reality, and the field of sales continues to provide the tempering for Jim's extensive educational background. That background includes:

- An undergraduate degree in business and education.
- A Masters Degree in Marketing.
- Ph.D. work in Management.
- Hundreds of hours of organizational and industrial education.
- Teaching sales and marketing as an Assistant Professor of Business at the college level.
- Guest lecturer on marketing at the University of Karachi in Karachi, Pakistan.

His sales background includes:

- SELLING on the retail level for the Allied Corporation.
- SELLING communication systems for AT&T. He was also a sales trainer and a sales training manager within the Bell System.
- SELLING business computer systems for the Burroughs Corporation. He was also an account and sales manager for Burroughs.

Sales, sales training, and speaking on sales have taken Jim literally around the world. The companies he has done sales training for include:

Hyatt Hotels
Northwestern Mutual Life
Hawkeye Bank and Trust
MetLife/Healthcare Network
Sheraton Hotels
Commerce Banking Group
Anheuser-Busch Companies
Ritz-Carlton Hotels
Performax Systems International
4-H of America
American Oriental Imports
and many others

In the area of human performance, Jim's working knowledge has been enhanced by the work he and his firms have done with professional athletes and coaches. Through personal experience, Jim has found that the world of sports has a lot to teach the business community about leadership, motivation, and even salesmanship.

Jim is the co-author of the Golfers Profile System from Performax Systems International, Inc., and was the founder of The Florida Golf Academy.

For additional information on:

* Keynote Speaking
* Sales Workshops and Seminars
* Sales Consulting
* Sales Management Training

you can contact Jim through Metamorphous Press, Inc., P.O. Box 10616, Portland, OR 97210; (503) 228-4972.

Metamorphous Press

Metamorphous Press is a publisher and distributor of books and other media providing resources for personal growth and positive changes. **Metamorphous Press** publishes and distributes leading edge ideas that help people strengthen their unique talents and discover that we are all responsible for our own realities.

Many of our titles have centered around NeuroLinguistic Programming, (NLP). NLP is an exciting, practical and powerful model of human communication systems that has been able to connect observable patterns of behavior and language to the processes that underlie them.

Metamorphous Press provides selections in many subject areas such as communication, health and fitness, education, business and sales, therapy, selections for young persons, and other subjects of general and specific interest. Our products are available in fine bookstores around the world. Among our Distributors for North America are:

Baker & Taylor   The Distributors
Bookpeople   Inland Book Co.
New Leaf Distributors   Moving Books, Inc.
Pacific Pipeline   Quality Books

For those of you overseas, we are distributed by:

Airlift (UK, Western Europe)
Specialist Publications (Australia)

New selections are added regularly and availability and prices change, so call for a current catalog or to be put on our mailing list. If you have difficulty finding our products in your favorite store or if you prefer to order by mail, we will be happy to make our books and other products available to you directly. Your involvement and your interest in what we do is always welcome. Please write or call at:

Metamorphous Press
P.O. Box 10616
Portland, OR 97210-0616
(503) 228-4972
TOLL FREE ORDER LINE
1-800-937-7771

Related Titles Available From
Metamorphous Press

Books

Best Seller
D. Forbes Ley $14.95
Beyond Selling
Dan Bagley & Edward Reese $19.95
The Challenge of Excellence
Scout Lee, Ed.D. & Jan Summers, Ed.D $16.95
The Excellence Principle
Scout Lee, Ed.D. $16.95
Fine Tune Your Brain
Genie Laborde $13.95
The Gentle Art of Verbal Self-Defense
Suzette Haden Elgin $6.95
Green Light Selling
Don Aspromonte & Diane Austin $14.95
How To Talk So Men Will Listen
Marian K. Woodall $7.95
Influencing With Integrity
Genie Laborde $12.95
**Magic of NLP Demystified: A Pragmatic Guide
To Communication And Change**
Byron Lewis & Frank Pucelik $9.95
Magic of Rapport
Jerry Richardson $12.95
Making The Message Clear
James Eicher $14.95
Making Your Mark: That's Marketing
Alyce Cornyn-Selby $7.50
**Modern Persuasion Strategies: The Hidden
Advantage in Selling**
Donald Moine & John Herd $19.95
Moving Up! Women and Leadership
Lois Borland Hart $13.95
90 Days To Communication Excellence
Genie Laborde $9.95
No Experience Necessary
Scott Nelson $12.95
**Performance Management: Creating The
Conditions For Results**
Michael McMaster $21.95

Phone Book
Richard Zarro & Peter Blum $9.95
Precision: A New Approach To Communication
Michael McMaster & John Grinder $18.95
Procrastinator's Success Kit
Alyce Cornyn-Selby $9.95
Results On Target
Bruce Dillman $12.50
Speaking To A Group
Marian K. Woodall $15.95
Thinking On Your Feet
Marian K. Woodall $9.95
Unlimited Selling Power
Donald Moine & Kenneth Lloyd $12.95
Whatever Happened To Teamwork?
Alyce Cornyn-Selby $7.50
Why Do Winners Win?
Alyce Cornyn-Selby $7.50

Audio Tapes

Building Better Relationships
Tim Hallbom & Suzi Smith $7.95
Connecting: Sales Rapport Thru NLP
W. Scott Phillips & Jim Mantock $65.00
Dynamics of Effective Presentation
John Grinder $110.00
Get Around To It
Paul Scheele $24.95
**Get Control of Your Money For
Control of Your Life**
Fred Waddell & Bernard Cleveland $9.95
Memory Supercharger
Paul Scheele $14.95
Prosperity
Paul Scheele $24.95
Sales Leap
Paul Scheele $24.95
Secrets Of Captivating Sales Presentations
Donald Moine & Kenneth Lloyd $100.00
Self Sabotage
Alyce Cornyn-Selby $9.95
Skills For Effective Presentation
John Grinder $110.00

Ten Minute Supercharger
Paul Scheele $14.95
Thinking On Your Feet
Marian K. Woodall $19.95

Video Tapes

Strategy For Responding To Criticism
Steve & Connirae Andreas $50.00

These are only a few of the titles we offer, and new titles are added regularly. Prices and availability may change without notice. Call or write us for current catalog information.

Metamorphous Press
P.O. Box 10616 - Dept. K
Portland, OR 97210-0616
(503) 228-4972
TOLL FREE ORDER LINE
1-800-937-7771